Praise for *What Makes You Come Alive: A Spiritual Walk with Howard Thurman*

"If you have been searching for an engaging introduction to Howard Thurman, here it is. Lerita Coleman Brown has spent so much time learning about his life, absorbing his work, and trusting his guidance that she has made his wisdom her own. This book makes good on its central promise: in her hands, it is not a book *about* Howard Thurman; it is a spiritual walk *with* him. Accept her invitation to take that walk, and the healing won't stop with your spirit. Your body, mind, and heart will be restored as well."

—**Barbara Brown Taylor,** author of *An Altar in the World* and *Holy Envy*

"Lerita Coleman Brown's *What Makes You Come Alive* invites all who will to step onto the seeker's path, to engage in the personal search for an 'ordinary mystic,' and to experience the joy of encountering Howard Thurman."

—**Catherine Meeks**, PhD, executive director of Absalom Jones Episcopal Center for Racial Healing and coauthor of *Passionate for Justice: Ida B. Wells as Prophet for Our Time*

"*What Makes You Come Alive* is a wonderful book on multiple levels. Lerita Coleman Brown has written an excellent introduction to Howard Thurman, one of the most important mystics of our time. But this book also stands as a beautiful and insightful survey of contemplative wisdom in its own right."

—**Carl McColman**, author of *Eternal Heart* and *The Big Book of Christian Mysticism*

"Howard Thurman counseled and trained many civil rights luminaries—Martin Luther King Jr., Bayard Rustin, John Lewis, and Pauli Murray among them. In *What Makes You Come Alive*, Lerita Coleman Brown invites us to join her for a spiritual walk and conversation with Howard Thurman. Enhanced with practical exercises, reflection questions, and 'spiritual steps,' this wise, engaging, and deeply insightful book is a genuine treasure. I have gleaned many invaluable lessons from it."

—**Jan Willis**, professor of religion, emerita, at Wesleyan University, Middletown, CT, and author of *Dreaming Me: Black, Baptist and Buddhist*

"In this wonderful and timely book, Lerita Coleman Brown not only introduces the reader to the spiritual virtuoso Howard Thurman; she skillfully connects his teachings to her own experience as a psychology professor, spiritual director, and retreat leader. Simply and elegantly written, this wonderful distillation of Howard Thurman's profound wisdom includes questions and guides at the end of each chapter that invite readers into their own creative encounter with their truth, mystery, and the love of God. I highly recommend *What Makes You Come Alive* to churches, religious and educational institutions, and spiritual seekers everywhere who are looking for an inward journey that finds its home in the world of nature, people, and things."

—**Walter Earl Fluker,** editor and director of the Howard Thurman Papers Project and Dean's Professor of Spirituality, Ethics, and Leadership at Candler School of Theology

"*What Makes You Come Alive* opens many windows into the legacy of Howard Thurman, one of the most important religious thinkers of twentieth-century America, an inspiration to Martin Luther King Jr. and countless thousands of others. For both longtime admirers and those wishing to know more about Thurman, take a spiritual walk with Lerita Coleman Brown in this marvelous book. It brings Howard Thurman alive, and may work the same magic for you."

—**Peter Eisenstadt,** author of *Against the Hounds of Hell: A Life of Howard Thurman*

"This book is the most extensive portrayal of Howard Thurman's influence upon a spiritual seeker. The 'walk' with Thurman and Lerita Brown Colman invites readers to explore their own religious experiences that guide living with deeper meaning and fulfillment. Abundant insights are given for a lifelong journey."

—**Luther E. Smith Jr.,** PhD, professor emeritus, Candler School of Theology, Emory University

"Lerita Coleman Brown offers us a lucid, informative, and inspiring book focused on the life and writings of Howard Thurman and how they have influenced her own life. She provides us with many of his profound insights into a liberating, socially active, and mystical spirituality that makes us come alive. In doing so, she weaves spiritual and racial justice into a tapestry of sacred activism."

—**Rev. Tilden Edwards**, PhD, founder and senior fellow of the Shalem Institute for Spiritual Formation

"This book is a spiritual page-turner. And yet no one will race through it because some passages carry scriptural valence and demand pausing for personal application. Even for those of us familiar with the genius of Howard Thurman and who also have a contemplative practice, Lerita Coleman Brown reveals new depths of spirituality befitting her lifelong experience as a scholar and spiritual mentor. There is more here than her being spiritually profound; she is spiritually, biographically, *and* autobiographically revelatory. I felt conscripted into Thurman's nonviolent, liberative movement."

—**Ed Bacon**, Episcopal priest and author of 8 *Habits of Love*

"What an immense gift from scholar, spiritual director, and contemplative Dr. Lerita Coleman Brown! In *What Makes You Come Alive* she offers a whole new generation ageless wisdom from one of the spiritual greats of the twentieth century—and right on time. Take a spiritual walk with Dr. Howard Thurman and find a guiding light to center down with the Holy One and become acquainted with your inner authority for sacred activism. This book is a treasure for all

those yearning for spiritual sustenance in our exhausting and spiritually malnourished times."
—**Lisa Colón DeLay**, author of *The Wild Land Within* and host of the *Spark My Muse* podcast

"Lerita Coleman Brown has done a magnificent job of demystifying the profound, multilayered wisdom of Howard Thurman in a way that has not been done before. She invites every single reader into a personally accessible, intimate encounter with Thurman's teachings, freshly relevant in our twenty-first-century world."
—**Arthur C. Jones**, professor emeritus of music, culture, and psychology, University of Denver, and founder of The Spirituals Project

"This book guides the reader through Howard Thurman's life and philosophy just as Thurman himself guided people in mentoring them: gently, with ample use of stories and real-life situations, and with probing questions at the end to point one toward wisdom."
—**Paul Harvey**, distinguished professor of history, University of Colorado

"Lerita Coleman Brown offers her readers the generous gift of guidance through Howard Thurman's wisdom. Weaving in her own experiences, the text becomes a sacred conversation about what it means to be fully human. In a world deadened by speed and consumption, *What Makes You Come*

Alive is a reminder of how a heart attuned to the Divine can bring grace to the challenges we experience and love to all who dwell on the edges. This should be required reading for anyone interested in spiritual direction or mysticism."

—**Christine Valters Paintner**, PhD, online abbess of Abbey of the Arts and author of *Breath Prayer*

"To read this book is to walk with Howard Thurman and Lerita Coleman Brown through sacred encounters with nature, to unearth the religion of Jesus, to center down into your soul and the heart of God, to be inspired toward sacred activism, and to discover a liberating spirituality. Howard Thurman inspired and mentored many great women and men during his lifetime and beyond. Read this book and you may discover that you are indeed an 'ordinary mystic' and that you have the courage to 'follow the grain of your own wood' in this world."

—**Thomas J. Bushlack**, PhD, contemplative coach and consultant

"From her heartfelt connection to Howard Thurman's work, Lerita Coleman's book weaves Thurman's life story, his teachings, and her own story in a way that will make you 'come alive.' Through these lenses, she opens us to the religion of Jesus, to center down and explore the questions 'Who am I?' and 'To whom do I belong?' Drawing on Thurman's words, Lerita poses reflection questions and spiritual steps that invite us to explore our inner authority and to imagine a more grounded, liberating spirituality.

This can serve all of us, the disinherited and the powerful, to discern our way of sacred activism for today's polarized world."

—**Ravi Verma**, retreat leader and past council chair of Spiritual Directors International

"*What Makes You Come Alive* is a warm welcome to meet African American mystic Howard Thurman and to explore our spiritual lives from a contemporary contemplative perspective. Brown's personal reflections on her encounters with Thurman's wisdom and legacy, and specific invitations for readers to connect with the many places we each meet Spirit, make for an intimate and soul-nourishing read."

—**Debonee Morgan**, executive director of Zeitgeist

"While no one can walk our path for us, Howard Thurman reminds us that the Spirit blazes the trail and guides our feet. Through Lerita's deeply meaningful reflections on his life, we remember how God fans the flames of our hearts and kindles our desire for wholeness. This book is a powerful encouragement to trust, to love, and to take steps toward aliveness."

—**Rev. Dr. Stuart Higginbotham**, rector at Grace Episcopal Church, Gainesville, Georgia, and author of *The Heart of a Calling*

"Dr. Lerita Coleman Brown's writing brings a whole new offering to the canon on Howard Thurman. While others have interpreted his writings, Brown brings forth his softness in early relationships, his compassion in world concerns, and his fierceness in sacred activism. Brown crosses the boundaries of time to intimately engage with Howard Thurman like never before."

—**Cassidy Hall**, author, filmmaker, and podcast host of *Contemplating Now* and *Encountering Silence*

"What Makes You Come Alive is an invitation to move into wholeness and authentic relationship, leaving nothing and no one behind. Through her skillful introduction to Thurman, Lerita Coleman Brown calls us to inner freedom, personal spiritual renewal, and a sacred type of activism of love and respect for all. This is not just a book about a historical figure from the past. It is a field guide to living wisdom here and now, offered right when it is needed."

—**Kevin M. Johnson**, university professor and cohost of the *Encountering Silence* podcast

WHAT MAKES YOU COME ALIVE

WHAT MAKES YOU COME ALIVE

A SPIRITUAL WALK WITH HOWARD THURMAN

LERITA COLEMAN BROWN

 Broadleaf Books

Minneapolis

WHAT MAKES YOU COME ALIVE
A Spiritual Walk with Howard Thurman

The meditation "The Inward Sea" on pp. 141-42 is reprinted with
permission of the Thurman Estate.

Cover design: Brad Norr

Print ISBN: 978-1-5064-7465-6
eBook ISBN: 978-1-5064-7466-3

To the memory of Leroy Frank Coleman,
precious brother and first spiritual companion

CONTENTS

CHAPTER 1

ICON IN A CAMPGROUND

BECOME ACQUAINTED WITH HOWARD THURMAN

Don't ask what the world needs. Ask what makes you come alive and go do that, because what the world needs is more people who have come alive.

—Howard Thurman

My friend Harriet and I trudge across the clay dirt that leads to the grounds of the Wild Goose Festival, an outdoor gathering of "Spirit, Justice, Music, and Art" in the North Carolina mountains. At the entrance we notice two dirt roads that meet to form a circle around the main stage and that rapidly fill with pedestrian traffic. Dusty in the mornings and muddy after a daily afternoon rain, the path can be treacherous. Along one side of the path, vendors sell food, jewelry, pottery, and clothes. Dotted on the other side sit bannered tables representing various nonprofit organizations and seminary programs, and volunteers offer grocery tote bags, pens, and pamphlets to promote their causes. Everywhere large oak and birch trees give shade to the audiences that fan out in front of tented stages.

It is 2017, and as two African American women, Harriet and I don't quite know what to expect from the weekend. The day before, I presented a brief talk on Howard Thurman as part of a pre-festival event. Surprised by the large, mostly white audience that gathered in an old revival-style tent on the banks of the shimmering French Broad River, I was even more astonished by the crowd who thronged the stage afterward. Where could they find out more about this Howard Thurman? Why had they never heard of him?

Now as Harriet and I stand in the sweltering July heat, a woman rolls up in a golf cart shuttle designed to help festivalgoers get around the grounds. "You ladies need a ride somewhere?" she inquires.

"No, thanks," I reply. We chat a bit, and we learn the woman's name is Bec. I tell her about the talk on Howard Thurman I gave yesterday, and that I will give another presentation about Thurman and the mystical heart of nonviolence in an hour. The library tent is not far from here, though, I say, so we can walk. Bec signals to us to stay put, then speeds away on her golf cart and into the campground.

A few minutes later she returns, and on the seat of the golf cart beside her sits an icon-style painting of Howard Thurman. I peer at the painted canvas into the face of Howard Thurman as he appears on the cover of his book *Meditations of the Heart*. He wears a gray ministerial robe with a white shirt and royal blue tie. A thin layer of jet-black hair crowns his head above a smooth face, and deep folds of wisdom frame his classic moustache. The artist has captured his penetrating eyes with startling precision. Circling his head, a rainbow of yellow, green, pink, and red half-moon swirls forms a halo of sorts. At the bottom of the portrait, a pink background filled with green strokes creates a forest scene, with hints of trees and birds.

Bec tells us she painted it herself, and she thrusts the painting into my hands. "Here. This is for you."

I stand there, dumbfounded. Who is this woman? Why has she painted a portrait of Howard Thurman—and why has she brought it with her to this campground in North Carolina?

Bec putters off in her little golf cart before I can ask her all my questions. Harriet and I stand there on the path for a moment, marveling at the icon of Thurman in my hands. I know a bit about the folklore surrounding the Wild Goose Festival—the talk that a holy coincidence could happen at any moment. In Celtic spirituality, geese represent the Holy Spirit, and I find that in my experience as a spiritual director and companion, Spirit orchestrates events without warning. Even with that awareness, I remain incredulous. Is this a coincidence, or is this some manifestation of the spirit of Howard Thurman? If the latter, what does he want?

I look more closely at the painting of "Saint Howard Thurman," initialed by Bec. I still can't fathom why Bec painted this portrait, or why we happened to cross paths that morning. Harriet and I shake our heads and smile. Then we walk together toward my next event about Thurman, under the broad canopy of trees.

DISCOVERING HOWARD THURMAN

Seven years earlier I was searching for a final project to fulfill the requirements for my spiritual direction and companioning training program. My frustration was growing. I wanted to research and write about a holy person—someone I could get to know, whose work spoke to my soul and whose spiritual evolution I could observe. But no one whose work I had read thus far excited me. The mystics we were reading lived hundreds of years ago, primarily in Europe—although there was a passing reference to an Asian Buddhist or Sufi poet. Each one lived in a religious community, often in a monastery or convent isolated from the neighborhoods and daily routines I was familiar with. I wondered if becoming a monk or nun was the only way to commune with God and live a holy life.

My interest in spirituality had begun many years ago, during college. Over the years, I read Catholic mystics like St. Theresa of Ávila and St. John of the Cross; dabbled in Thomas Merton; studied Quaker mystics George Fox, Thomas Kelly, and John Woolman and Sufi mystics Rabia, Rumi, and Hafiz; and enjoyed the work of Henri Nouwen. Having perused the writings of dozens of spiritual teachers, I remained especially curious about "ordinary mystics," as Marsha Sinetar refers to them. Ordinary mystics are regular people who sense the presence of God, hear a guiding voice, or have a transcendent experience of oneness. Mysticism, writes Father Albert Haase, means "living with a sensitivity to the divine presence and responding to God's ardent longing and enthusiastic invitation to a deeper relationship at this very moment: in a burning bush as happened to Moses, in the tiny whisper of a sound as Elijah experienced, in the call out of hiding like Zacchaeus." In whatever manner an experience of God occurs, a radical inner transformation frequently accompanies it. This shift may include becoming less self-centered and more focused on God, other people, and the larger world.

Sometimes I wondered whether I might be an ordinary mystic—and perhaps you do too.

Do mystics sometimes live outside of religious communities, practicing contemplation in the middle of normal life? And what about African or African American mystics? They must exist somewhere in the history of the world, I thought. So why hadn't I encountered any Black contemplatives in my studies? Why was I often the only Black person in the room at spiritual direction trainings and workshops or on silent retreats? I prayed to Spirit to direct me to a wisdom teacher in whom I could see my psychological, racial, and spiritual reality reflected.

When I shared my concerns with an African American clergy friend and pastoral counselor, Joshua, he looked at me in disbelief. "You mean you haven't heard of Howard Thurman?" he asked. "He is an American treasure!" No, I had never heard of him. Why wasn't his name mentioned when people spoke about Christian mystics—even contemporary ones, like Thomas Merton or Mother Theresa?

Joshua recommended a few Thurman books for me to read. When I opened the pages of *Meditations of the Heart* and later *With Head and Heart: The Autobiography of Howard Thurman*, I felt an immediate sense of spiritual kinship. Then, as I delved more deeply into Howard Thurman and his work, I was overcome with shock and grief. Our lives, separated as they were by more than fifty years, had overlapped. In the early 1970s, Thurman and I had both lived in the San Francisco Bay area, where he actively lectured and spoke. But I had heard nothing about him. Throughout my adult life I had attended predominately Black churches across the country, and I had participated in many spiritual retreats. But his name had remained absent from all those conversations. Why had I never encountered his work or been introduced to his writing?

I had finally met my spiritual mentor. To read a Thurman book, or listen to his deep baritone voice, is to understand why people refer to his writings, sermons, and lectures as *living* wisdom. More than forty years after his death, Thurman's words continue to feed me, my spirit, and any hearts or souls willing to listen.

MAKES YOU COME ALIVE

"Once, when I was seeking the advice of Howard Thurman and talking to him at some length about what needed to be done in the world, he interrupted me," writes Gil Bailie in the acknowledgments of his book *Violence Unveiled*. Thurman replied, "Don't ask what the world needs. Ask what makes you come alive and go do that, because what the world needs is more people who have come alive."

The quotation now appears on everything from Instagram posts to mugs and posters. While it is popular enough to risk losing its meaning, that quotation remains emblematic of Thurman's work. Howard Thurman observed an aliveness in all living things, despite their physical appearance. During stark winters, when dead leaves cling to skeletal trees and flowering perennials die back, life is still at work underground. When spring arrives, as new tree seedlings blast up through hard soil and leaves burst out of tree buds, our spirits are similarly stirred and awakened. In a moment we glimpse an inner shift from emptiness to fullness, from stagnation to animation.

Already well known in select seminaries and at some historically Black colleges and universities, Thurman's writings and sermons are finally filtering outside of academic and theological circles. In a time of chaos and uncertainty, when it feels as if the world is upside down, his spiritual insights resonate. One of Thurman's lifelong quests was to inspire hope, to remind young and old human spirits that they must not allow circumstances to overcome them. During those months after the Wild Goose Festival, I had noticed an increasing demand for lectures and retreats on Thurman. I soon realized that a few retreats and lectures each year would not suffice for the thousands of spiritual pilgrims thirsty for living water and nourishment for their starving souls.

Like Bec in her golf cart, who had offered me an icon of Howard Thurman, I wanted to give others a portrait of Thurman—an introduction to what his living wisdom might mean for spiritual seekers and ordinary mystics. It became evident that Spirit was issuing me an invitation to share what I had learned from Thurman. This book about Howard Thurman's living wisdom is for spiritual seekers everywhere, and it stems from that call.

WHO WAS HOWARD THURMAN?

Howard Thurman is known as the spiritual adviser to Martin Luther King Jr. and other leaders of the civil rights movement. But as my study of him deepened, I discovered that this label doesn't begin to represent the full breadth of his contributions. His quest for a profound experience of the presence of God, of connection to all living things, serves as a model for any spiritual seeker venturing into uncharted territory. Thurman's witness, through his life, writings, lectures, and sermons, serves as sustenance for the journey. Before we begin our walk with Howard Thurman as our spiritual companion, let's consider the contours of his life.

Dr. Howard Washington Thurman was born on November 18, 1899, near Palm Beach, Florida. Shortly after his birth, his family moved to Daytona Beach, Florida, where Howard spent his early years with his parents, two sisters, and maternal grandmother, Nancy Ambrose. Saul Thurman, his father, worked as a laborer on the railroad and often spent the weekdays away from the family. Even though his wife, Alice, and his mother-in-law actively participated in a local Baptist church, Saul maintained a certain suspicion about organized religion. He read a great deal and did not attend church.

One day when young Howard was seven years old, his father arrived home from work very ill with pneumonia. Saul Thurman suffered for about four days before he died. Howard, present in the bedroom, beheld his father's last breath. Because Saul Thurman was not a church member, several local ministers refused to officiate his funeral. Finally one traveling preacher agreed, but in his eulogy he condemned Saul Thurman to hell because he was not a churchgoer. This incident baffled young Howard. He began to wonder about Christianity and how a minister who knew nothing about his father could castigate him in this way. Howard vowed that once he reached adulthood, he would never join a church.

This pledge was short-lived. Howard's mystical experiences in nature and his burning desire to teach, lead, and uplift the human spirit were undeniable, and these longings constantly tugged at his heart. Later in his life he cofounded an interracial, interdenominational church designed to reflect his sense of what God desired: community or oneness for all people, for all creation. It became a sanctuary for those who sought spiritual renewal and change in the larger society. With literature, art, liturgical dance, meditation, and phenomenal sermons, Thurman created a worship experience in which those in attendance felt the presence of God.

After his father's death, a grieving and lonely Howard spent much of his time outside alone. Silence and solitude offered solace to Thurman, and in nature he frequently experienced the presence of God, or oneness. He sensed that something larger and more expansive than him underlay the universe. He also spent time reading to Grandma Nancy, a formerly enslaved woman turned midwife and laundress. She shared stories with Howard and modeled for him how a person of God thrives in a hostile world. One way that she survived the horrors of slavery was to remember what a traveling enslaved preacher told her and other enslaved people each time he visited: that each of them was a holy child of God. Grandma Nancy wanted young Howard to internalize this belief, to make it central to his identity. In many ways, she was attempting to inoculate him from the oppressive circumstances in which he lived.

In the early 1900s, in Daytona Beach, Florida, African American children were only permitted to receive formal schooling to the seventh grade and were excluded from a high school education. Thurman's community came together to ensure that this very bright adolescent received private tutoring so he could earn the necessary certificate to enroll in a residential high school. Thurman graduated at the top of his class from the Florida Baptist Academy in Jacksonville. Exhausted by both schoolwork and the job he maintained to cover most of his school expenses, Howard actually collapsed before his valedictory address at graduation.

As high school valedictorian, Thurman qualified for a tuition fellowship to Morehouse College. In 1919, he began his studies at Morehouse, exploring a wide array of subjects but focusing primarily on economics and sociology. During the summer prior to his senior year, he took courses in philosophy at Columbia University in New York. He again graduated as valedictorian. A rumor circulated that he had read every book in the college's library. Thurman was then admitted to Colgate Rochester Theological Seminary and again graduated as the valedictorian of his seminary class.

In seminary, he heard a message about what his future role might hold from his beloved seminary professor, George Cross. With a most somber tone, Cross, who was white, shared that while he had no idea what it was like to be a Negro, he recommended Thurman focus his energies on feeding the spiritual hunger of the masses. Cross said he'd understand if Thurman felt like he needed to devote his efforts to the racial struggle, but such social issues are ephemeral, he told him. With his keen intellect, Thurman could make a significant contribution to the field of spirituality.

Thurman received this message from Cross with ambivalence. On the one hand, he heard that his vocation may be to support others in spiritual formation: to connect them with God, and to use spiritual practices like silence, solitude, and contact with nature to feed their yearning for God. That calling resonated with him. But he was also keenly aware of the suffering of his people—Black folks who were at the time called "coloreds," and later "Negroes"—who were living under the repressive and damaging atmosphere of Jim Crow and segregation. Was he simply to ignore the realities of racial injustice? Thurman would eventually find ways to weave spirituality and racial justice together into a tapestry of sacred activism. Thurman firmly believed God always moves us to greater unity through many forms of reconciliation.

One week after graduating from seminary, Howard Thurman married Katie Laura Kelley in a ceremony at dawn at her home in La Grange, Georgia. Katie, a graduate of Spelman High School and the teacher's course at Spelman College, obtained training in social work prior to their marriage. She worked extensively with the Anti-Tuberculosis Association in Atlanta before accepting a position to direct a municipal health department. Immediately following the wedding breakfast, they boarded a train to Oberlin, Ohio. They would welcome a daughter, Olive Katherine Thurman, in October 1927.

Howard Thurman began his pastoral duties in 1926 at Mt. Zion Baptist Church in Oberlin, Ohio. During a conference, he purchased a book by Quaker mystic Rufus Jones, and he was so moved by what he read that he arranged for a semester of study with Jones at Haverford College. This was the beginning of Thurman's formal study of mysticism. The silence, stillness, and solitude that he was attracted to as a boy were serving as powerful tools in spiritual growth and development. After his study with Jones, Howard Thurman returned to a joint professorship in religion at Morehouse and Spelman Colleges in Atlanta, where he also became director of spiritual life. Due to the failing health of Katie, who had contracted tuberculosis, Thurman chose this position over many other professional opportunities. Katie died on December 31, 1930. Thurman was now a widower with a young child and living in the racially repressive atmosphere of Atlanta.

During the late fall of 1931, he shared a speaking event with Sue Bailey, a woman of outstanding intellect with a zest for life. She attended the same Spelman preparatory schools and colleges as Katie Kelley and later graduated from Oberlin College with degrees in music and liberal arts. Active in the YWCA, she developed programs for girls and created music curricula for many southern Black schools. When they married on June 12, 1932, their wedding reflected their taste in poetry and scripture, music, and silence. Howard and Sue formed a solid partnership and collaborated on spiritual, religious, and intellectual endeavors. During their nearly forty-nine years of marriage, Sue would lead a number of independent projects for women and international students. Their daughter, Anna Spencer Thurman, was born in October 1933.

A few months before their wedding, Howard Thurman had accepted an offer from his long-time mentor and then president of Howard University, Dr. Mordecai Wyatt Johnson, to assume a professorship and the role of dean at Rankin Chapel at Howard University. From 1932 to 1944, Thurman's influence grew through his teaching and poignant sermons, which he attributed to a certain leading of Spirit.

Using Negro spirituals as guides, Thurman blazed a path for others to follow with his writing and speaking about nonviolence in the 1920s and 1930s. Historian Anthony Siracusa highlights Thurman's contribution: "He began to sketch the outline of an ethical framework specifically for black liberation, and his analysis led him to the premier theme of his later work—the 'very Jesus contribution' he envisioned." Thurman uncovered, in the Gospels, clues to a nonviolent religion with a liberating spirituality. Thurman then led a pilgrimage to India and Burma and Ceylon, along with Sue Bailey Thurman and travel companions Edward and Phenola Carroll. They toured this area for nearly six months, presenting talks and lectures, leading discussion groups, and teaching spirituals to choirs. Toward the end they met with Mahatma Gandhi and discussed his notions of *ahimsa* (nonviolence) and *satyagraha* ("holding firmly to truth," or civil disobedience) in 1936. The spirited three-hour conversation with Gandhi emboldened Thurman's pursuit of and his fervor for understanding Jesus and the role of civility, compassion, and reconciliation in nonviolent direct action. Both Thurman's insights about Jesus and these Gandhian principles became central to the practice of nonviolent direct-action campaigns in the North and Midwest during the 1940s and 1950s. These early and sometimes interracial sit-ins led to the more widely known civil rights movement in the 1960s.

A few months before Thurman left for the trip to India, he published an article called "Good News for the Underprivileged." This piece would serve as the basis for his classic book *Jesus and the Disinherited*, in which Thurman draws a distinction between the religion of Jesus and contemporary forms of Christianity. He also poignantly discusses the liberating message that Jesus had for his fellow Jews, who at the time were all minorities in a Roman-occupied territory. Thurman suggests that Jesus's universal message is for all oppressed people—for all "who find themselves with their backs against the wall." Not long after its publication, a young Martin Luther King Jr. read *Jesus and the Disinherited* in a seminary course taught by one of Howard Thurman's former seminary classmates. It is said that Dr. King was so deeply inspired by the book that he carried it with him every time he marched.

While in India at the Khyber Pass, Howard and Sue Bailey Thurman received a vision, of sorts, about a fellowship where all people, regardless of race, ethnicity, or religion, could worship God together. They returned home, and a few years later, in 1944, Howard cofounded, with Dr. Alfred G. Fisk, the Church of the Fellowship of All Peoples in San Francisco. Known as Fellowship Church, the first intentionally interracial and interdenominational church in America included "at-large members," people who resided in other regions or outside of the United States. They supported the church financially and attended services during visits to the San Francisco area. When Thurman moved from co-pastor to pastor, he introduced a time for silence during the worship service. Subsequently he added a twenty- to thirty-minute meditation time before services. He wrote meditations especially for this time, which would come to compose one of his most popular books, *Meditations of the Heart*.

In 1953, Howard Thurman left Fellowship Church to become the first African American professor and dean of Marsh Chapel at Boston University. He continued to preach, lecture, and write. At the same time, Martin Luther King Jr. was finishing his doctoral work, and he listened to several of Thurman's sermons. On occasion Martin and Coretta met socially with the Thurmans.

Howard Thurman mentored many activists in the civil rights movement and would come to serve as its unofficial spiritual guide and adviser. Drawn to his presence and wisdom, many civil rights leaders—including Bayard Rustin, James Farmer, James Lawson, Jesse Jackson, and John Lewis—regularly sought Thurman for guidance and direction. Upon his retirement in 1965, he created and directed the Howard Thurman Educational Trust and served as minister emeritus at Fellowship Church. Thurman died in San Francisco in 1981, at the age of eighty-one.

SACRED ACTIVIST, SPIRITUAL GUIDE

The details that bring life to this brief biography of Howard Thurman will become clearer as we walk the spiritual path with him. Thurman's more than twenty books include meditations; essays on religion and the nature of people, mysticism, the spiritual disciplines, and segregation; and an autobiography. Thurman served as what we could call "a sacred activist," and he did so long before anyone had coined this term to describe the comingling of contemplation and action, spirituality and activism.

Merging political and social activism with spirituality produces less exhausting and more sustainable social progress. Sacred activism describes the daring actions of people grounded in Spirit. Religious and spiritual leaders like Moses, Jesus, Joan of Arc, Harriet Tubman, Sojourner Truth, Olive Schreiner, and George Fox might be considered sacred activists. Howard Thurman, Muriel Lester, and thousands of unknown people have utilized prayer and guidance from the Spirit of God to move dehumanized and oppressed people through the forces of evil. They are joined by better-known sacred activists like Mahatma Gandhi, Martin Luther King Jr., the Dalai Lama, Nelson Mandela, Thich Nhat Hanh, and Bishop Desmond Tutu. All have answered a sacred call and devoted their lives— their prayer, time, and energy—to the freedom of others. As we walk through Howard Thurman's liberating spirituality, we will see how God is always on the side of restoring community, or oneness, which requires dismantling systemic oppression and struggling for social justice, racial reconciliation, and care for the environment.

Having now read a great deal of Thurman's writings and having become one of the interpreters of Thurman's work through retreats, workshops, and lectures, I still like to dream about going for a walk with him. I imagine he would talk about many subjects: silence and solitude, nature, being a holy child of God, divine intervention, the religion of Jesus, mysticism, inner authority, and spiritual mentoring. These are the topics that constitute the chapters of this book. You might imagine each one as a stroll with Thurman—a conversation with him, and with me, about the deeply human and spiritual questions of life.

One reason Thurman's work necessitates careful study by contemporary activists is that social and political movements without a spiritual base are ultimately unsustainable. Thurman's work links the quest for the authentic self to mysticism, to religious experience that demands social change. We will learn from Howard Thurman that God is moving us toward unity and oneness, and that any attempts to usurp this cosmological certainty will eventually fail. He equips us with the expertise and practices to maintain a rich spiritual life, an aspect of our existence that we often ignore and rarely nurture. Thurman would insist that we need a rich spiritual life to feel alive. Rather than attempt to escape the world, Thurman suggests we "center down" for spiritual renewal. We may not be conscious that we are on a spiritual journey, but when crises and tribulations arise, a spiritual anchor is essential.

Historian Lerone Bennett describes Howard Thurman as a rare, multifaceted gem. "He had a great zest for food, flowers, fragrances and scents, and his days were filled with music and laughter," he writes. Thurman spoke with what Bennett calls "uncommon force and clarity" to his times: "He spoke at an in-depth level to racism in the church. He spoke to our fragmentation and spiritual hunger and lack of connectedness and relatedness. He spoke to our busyness, our internal noise, and our need to center down.... Standing in the midst of his idiom and reaching out to all other idioms—Christian and Jewish, Hindu and Buddhist, African, Asian, Indian, and European—[he] spoke to this crisis by calling us to the task of spiritual reconstruction."

This task—spiritual reconstruction—may sound daunting. But with Thurman's guidance, we walk together toward a reconstructed spirituality, remaining open to surprise gifts and knowing that we are not alone.

A few notes about what you will find in this book—first, about language. Please note that Thurman used the gender-biased and exclusive language of his era. Yet his life, spirituality, theology, and writings were most inclusive. If he were living today, I am most certain his writing would reflect the changes in our perspective.

And with regard to terminology for racial categories, throughout the book I will occasionally use the terms of Thurman's time period—such as "Negroes" and "colored people"—as a way to gesture toward the realities and language of his day.

To be more inclusive of many faith traditions, as Howard Thurman would have advocated, I use "Spirit" or "Indwelling Spirit" to denote the Christian term "Holy Spirit." I believe God instilled in each of us a "still small voice" to lead and guide us. Often manifesting as a "knowingness"—an urge, gut feeling, or intuition—it never leads us astray. Spirit is available for counsel and advice through the practice of discernment.

Spiritual seekers often ask me which of Thurman's books they should read first, or whether it would be better to read a compilation of his spiritual wisdom. To distill the best of Howard Thurman is a challenge. I hope, though, between these book covers, you will receive a taste of some aspects of Thurman's spiritual teachings that makes you long for more. If so, you can follow up with a more thorough reading of one of his texts; a recommended reading list appears at the back of the book, with readings associated with each chapter. For deeper reflection or conversation, questions are available at the end of each chapter. In addition, spiritual practices allow you to apply Thurman's wisdom to your daily life. The epigraphs at the beginning of each chapter are from Thurman's writings, with the exception of chapter 9.

On that steamy July day at the Wild Goose Festival in North Carolina, I carried Bec's painting of Howard Thurman along to my next event. Sitting it on a chair next to the podium, I delighted in the idea that his spirit might be present among us. There I found another crowd of people eager to learn about him. Together we were inspired by his mystical approach to nonviolence, his encounters with the Presence in all things, and his model as a sacred activist.

As Harriet and I walked back to where we were staying after that conversation, I meditated on all that I had already learned from Thurman, and all that I had yet to learn.

REFLECTION QUESTIONS

- Who or what feeds your spiritual hunger?
- If you could take a contemplative walk with someone from history or contemporary life, who would it be? Why?

SPIRITUAL STEPS

- Name some people or activities that make you come alive. Spend some time becoming more acquainted with people or activities that feed your soul—that make you feel alive. Incorporate these activities into your daily spiritual practice.

- Pay a visit to a spiritual location in your area that you are curious about. Take a tour of a Hindu temple, Buddhist monastery, or Christian cathedral. Note what makes these places feel sacred to you.

CHAPTER 2

OUR MINDS SEETHE WITH ENDLESS TRAFFIC

CENTER DOWN

We must learn to be quiet, to settle down in one spot for a spell. Sometime during each day, everything should stop and the art of being still must be practiced. For some temperaments, it will not be easy because the entire nervous system and body have been geared over the years to activity, to overt and tense functions. Nevertheless, the art of being still must be practiced until development and habit are sure.

—Howard Thurman, *Deep Is the Hunger*

Bec's painting of Howard Thurman sat against a wall in my living room for several months. Each time I passed it, I felt Thurman's eyes follow me. I sensed a questioning look from him and a deep silence. That painting had appeared as a talisman for me at a time when I needed it. It served as a reminder that I was called to help others encounter

Thurman as I had. Now he looked out at me from the painting as I walked past it on my way to the kitchen or to the front door and seemed to beckon me toward the silence that enveloped him—a silence that I had known and loved most of my life.

I'm not certain when my own love affair with silence and solitude began. I grew up with two brothers and, as the only girl in the family at the time, was granted my own bedroom. This personal sanctuary, away from the din of television, radio, and family life, offered a blanket of serenity. I spent many hours in silence looking out the window, reading, and daydreaming. Attendance at mass, as part of my parochial school elementary education, forged a link in my mind between silence and sacredness. When we entered the sanctuary, we were only allowed to whisper, and we sat quietly in our pews until an usher's signal to stand for the procession.

Later, in my adult years, I found the practice of sitting in silence in the morning—letting go of my thoughts and focusing inward to hear the voice of God—to relax and anchor me. This form of prayer did not remove all the stress of my life as a college professor. But I coped better with the stressors when I established a deep connection with my Creator through the habit of quieting my mind and stilling my heart.

The first of Thurman's books that I read was *Meditations of the Heart*, and in it I learned that Thurman championed silence, solitude, and stillness. The first section of *Meditations of the Heart*, titled "The Inward Sea," contains many meditations about silence: "Silence is a Door to God,"

"In Quiet One Discovers the Will of God," "A Lull in the Rhythm of Doing," "In the Moment of Pause, the Vision of God," and my favorite, "How Good to Center Down!" In this most instructive meditation, Howard Thurman notes how important it is to pause and connect with God: "How good it is to center down!" Thurman writes. "To sit quietly and see one's self pass by! The streets of our minds seethe with endless traffic; Our spirits resound with clashing, with noisy silences, While something deep within hungers and thirsts for the still moment and the resting lull."

Howard Thurman believed that a place deep within us yearns for moments of quiet serenity. Silence, stillness, and solitude: in our noise-filled lives, these bring peace, heal, strengthen, and facilitate spiritual growth. This belief is shared among mystics of many religious traditions. Writers from many faith traditions and spiritual philosophies such as Buddhism, Christianity, Judaism, Hinduism, Sufism, Taoism, Islam, and shamanism speak about the importance of these three pillars of the spiritual path.

When we intentionally center down in contemplative prayer and meditation, God reminds us of our unsevered bond. Invoking an inward quietness can aid the discernment process when facing life-altering decisions like a choice in medical treatment or a move to another city. To retreat silently even in our own homes or to escape from our daily routine even briefly—this allows answers to our questions to bubble up through an uncluttered mind.

As we walk quietly with Howard Thurman's wisdom on silence, stillness, and solitude, we grasp why he championed these spiritual disciplines. From his early discovery of meditation to his use of silence in worship services and for pastoral care, we witness with him the sheer healing power of silence. Quietness creates just enough space in the cacophony of our speeding thoughts for the voice of Spirit to break through. As we walk with Howard Thurman, we will see the many ways he befriended silence, stillness, and solitude—outside, in communal meditation, and in worship services and pastoral care.

THE YOUNG CONTEMPLATIVE

Some people believe that Howard Thurman was first introduced to meditation as an adult, during silent worship with the Quakers. Yet it's clear from his writings that Thurman began communing with God in the stillness of nature as a child. The reasons he was drawn to this spiritual practice carry more ominous undertones, however, than the sweet image of a child being quiet in nature might suggest. Thurman writes,

> I was a very sensitive child who suffered much from the violences of racial conflict. The climate of our town, Daytona Beach, Florida, was better than most Southern towns because of the influence of the tourists who wintered there. Nevertheless, life became more and more suffocating because of the fear of being brutalized, beaten, or otherwise outraged. In my effort to keep this fear from corroding my life and

making me seek relief in shiftlessness, I sought help from God. I found that the more I turned to prayer, to what I discovered in later years to be meditation, the more time I spent alone in the woods or on the beach, the freer became my own spirit and the more realistic became my ambition to get an education.

Quietness offered young Howard respite from the racist fury of the Jim Crow South. It also consoled him as he grieved the loss of his father at age seven. In nature's stillness, he discovered the presence of God as a balm. "When I was young, I found more companionship in nature than I did among people. The woods befriended me," he writes. "The quiet, even the danger, of the woods provided my rather lonely spirit with a sense of belonging that did not depend on human relationships. I was usually with a group of boys as we explored the woods, but I tended to wander away to be alone for a time, for in that way I could sense the strength of the quiet and the aliveness of the woods."

Near his home, Howard Thurman spotted an oak tree that would become his favorite refuge. He returned to that tree to share his joys and sorrows with it, and he felt that the tree truly understood him. Here, under its branches, Howard Thurman began a practice of meditation. Meditation continued to serve as a form of spiritual renewal, a source of vitality throughout Thurman's life, and allowed him to express the considerable wisdom he acquired in quietness.

It's unclear whether Howard Thurman meditated regularly when he attended high school at the Florida Baptist

Academy or Morehouse College. But one of his classmates at Rochester Seminary, Kenneth Cober, writes about participating in weekly meditation sessions that Thurman led there. "Thus began one of my most memorable friendships," writes Cober. "I believe that no one outside of my own family has made a greater contribution to my thinking and my life. About once a week, Howard would invite the boys on our floor to meet in his room for a devotional experience which he led. He would read some scriptures, interpret what he read, and pray. Then we had a period of meditation interspersed by other vocal prayers."

SILENCE AND STILLNESS AS A FORM OF PRAYER

Spiritual seekers on retreat and those who seek spiritual direction often lament to me that their prayers remain unanswered. They tell me about how much they pray and how disappointed they are that their pleas go unanswered. Sometimes I ask them, "Well, what have you heard?"

Listening is also prayer. When I explain to retreatants or spiritual companions that prayer is not a monologue but a dialogue and that I believe our Creator wants to commune with us, they are often surprised. Like me, they were taught specific forms of prayer, such as petitionary or intercessory prayer, prayers of gratitude, and prayers of contrition. To pause, be still, and listen? They're not sure that even counts. I often remind people that the words *silent* and *listen* contain exactly the same letters, just rearranged. One must be silent to truly listen.

Like many spiritual seekers, I now consider listening to God in silence and solitude vital. Personal prayers like "Help me, Jesus" or "Lord, I could really use some help down here" are just as effective as repeated recitations of standard prayers or prayers in a book. Further, the answer to a prayer may not appear in the form and at the time we expect. Howard Thurman encourages us to slow down, pause, be quiet, if only for a few moments, and connect with eternal wisdom.

Unfortunately, many Christians associate contemplative practices like meditation, centering prayer, or silent retreats with Eastern religions or philosophies and then categorically reject them. Yet early Christians fled into the desert to escape persecution and to experience the power of solitude, silence, and stillness. These early desert mothers and fathers heard holy wisdom in silence and served as the first Christian spiritual directors and companions. They urged those who came seeking spiritual guidance to maintain a regular practice of silence and solitude, similar to meditation or contemplative prayer. Later, many Christian contemplative practices moved to monasteries and private hermitages. Practiced by nuns and monks for centuries, centering prayer and Christian meditation spread to millions beyond cloistered communities—to retreat centers, meditation groups, prayer circles, support groups, and personal prayer times.

What contemplative prayer and different forms of meditation—including insight, mindfulness, transcendental, and vipassana meditation—have in common is an attempt

WHAT MAKES YOU COME ALIVE
to reduce the inner chatter. When the mind is quieted and

to reduce the inner chatter. When the mind is quieted and the heart stilled, we often discover physical, emotional, psychological, and spiritual healing. When we rest the mind, we can access other forms of consciousness. What distinguishes religious or Christian meditation from other forms, though, is its focus on God, paired with the desire for a deep, ongoing, intimate relationship with the Creator.

Howard Thurman notes that Jesus is the perfect role model for Christians who seek silence and solitude. Often Jesus took time away outside in the early morning stillness or late in the evening when the crowds dispersed so that he could pray alone and in the quiet. Thurman writes this of Jesus's times in prayer: "This was the time for the long breath, when all the fragments left by the commonplace, when all the hurts and the big aches could be absorbed, and the mind could be freed of the immediate demand, when voices that had been quieted by the long day's work could once more be heard, when there could be the deep sharing of the innermost secrets and the laying bare of the heart and mind."

Like Jesus, Howard Thurman, and other mystics, contemporary contemplatives pray in silence, stillness, and solitude because they believe that quiet listening in the presence of God is as essential as eating and drinking. Thurman writes,

> We must find sources of strength and renewal for our own spirits, lest we perish. There is widespread recognition of the need for refreshment of the mind and the heart. It is very much in order to make certain concrete suggestions in this regard. . . . If possible,

find a comfortable chair or quiet spot where one may engage in nothing. There is no reading of a book or a paper, no thinking of the next course of action, no rejecting of remote or immediate mistakes of the past, no talk. One is engaged in doing nothing at all except being still.... The first step in the discovery of sources of strength and renewal is to develop the art of being still, physical and mental cessation from churning.

LIVING FROM THE STILLNESS WITHIN

Howard Thurman continued to cultivate his relationship with silence and solitude during his time with the Religious Society of Friends. He discovered Quaker mystic Rufus Jones's book *Finding the Trail of Life* and found it stoked his burning desire to know more about the power of silence and mysticism. His semester of study with Jones gave him a sense of direction intellectually and strengthened his bond with the presence of God.

For more than four hundred years, a vibrant Quaker commitment to the mystical practice of silence has persisted. Many people remain unaware of the contributions of Quakers to American history and religion. Staunch promoters of the "still small voice," Quakers believe that everyone carries the divine light of God within them and that we are all equal regardless of title or socioeconomic status. They believe that God speaks ceaselessly to us and that quietness and stillness are prerequisites for hearing the soft, gentle, wordless communication of God. Yet for Quakers, being contemplative is not enough; they assume that actions emerging from the silence should facilitate the end of social injustices and the creation of a more benevolent world. As advocates of peace and equality, many Quakers participated in the Underground Railroad, assisting thousands in escaping slavery.

As part of his study of mysticism, Howard Thurman attended Quaker meetings and sat in the silence that characterizes unscripted forms of Quaker worship. In a 1951 sermon on the strength of silence in corporate worship, later excerpted in *Visions of a Better World: Howard Thurman's Pilgrimage to India*, Thurman speaks of his personal experience with group silence during a traditional Quaker meeting:

> *Nobody said a word . . . just silence. Silence. Silence. And in that silence I felt as though all of them were on one side and I was on the other side, by myself, with my noise. And every time I would try to get across the barrier, nothing happened. I was just Howard Thurman. And then . . . I don't know when it happened, how it happened, I wish I could tell you, but somewhere in that hour I passed over the invisible line, and I became one with all the seekers. I wasn't Howard Thurman anymore; I was, I was a human spirit involved in a creative moment with human spirits, in the presence of God.*

As we saw in the previous chapter, Howard Thurman led a delegation on a pilgrimage to India in 1935–36. Toward the end of their six-month journey, they met with Mahatma Gandhi, who ended the fortuitous session with silence. The meeting both reinforced Thurman's dedication to a radical nonviolent movement in the United States and affirmed his belief in the importance of silence and the maintenance of a spiritual practice of quiet time.

Gandhi firmly held that asceticism and silence were key for feeding the soul and creating vitality. Thurman agreed with Gandhi's perspectives on those ideas, and upon his return to the United States, he reflected on the lack of a broad tradition of meditation or contemplative prayer in America. He observed that in India, meditation was as much a part of the culture as food and music were. In her biography of Howard Thurman, Elizabeth Yates notes his advocating for a regular meditation practice as early as the 1930s: "When the American learns to accept meditation as a necessary part of his way of life, it will have a powerful effect on him. Why? Because, by his nature, he will use it not as a flight from the world but as a time of renewal from which he will emerge stronger to face the world."

MEETING EACH OTHER IN SILENCE

Howard Thurman's early experiences with silence and his work with Rufus Jones molded his future thinking about silence. This was evident in how he structured worship services, attempting always to create time and space for still moments. When he first became a professor of religion and dean of the Rankin Chapel at Howard University, he spent hours in quietness, wondering how he could transform the chapel, where all large meetings were held, into a sacred space for worship. He searched for material, often writing poems and prose for this special time. Thurman punctuated the songs and sermons with ample time for silent prayer. Vespers services offered another opportunity for Thurman to read brief written meditations followed by several minutes of silence. He'd place moments of silence throughout his sermons to, as he put it, "allow the inspiration of the words to hold full sway."

At Fellowship Church, Thurman discovered that people desired more silence as part of the worship experience than churches usually afforded them. He reflects,

> In my opinion the most important part of the service is the period of meditation preceding the sermon. Here the congregation and the minister become still in the presence of God. This is the time when the innermost secrets of life are laid bare without pretense, when each one of us feels that he is in the presence of One who understands thoroughly and completely and in whose presence it is unnecessary to pretend anything. Out of the period of meditation there comes a high resolve, and a sense of being cleansed; sometimes there is the conviction of sin; but most often there rises hope and confidence for what awaits in the next turning of the road. At first the congregation experienced

some difficulty in being thrown so fully upon its own life and need without the customary voicing of the formal pastoral prayer. But more and more this quiet time has become a moment of rare and holy celebration.

Thurman began setting aside a few minutes prior to worship for congregants to gather for silence. The time was later expanded to twenty minutes, and it was for this time that Thurman wrote and read so many of his meditations, which were either handed out by ushers or included on the back of the weekly bulletin. After he added the silent meditation time prior to worship services, he noticed that requests for counseling appointments decreased. "This quiet period became one of the most dynamic sources of vitality in the life of the church," Thurman writes. "Again and again the quality of this first period of meditation would carry over into the briefer second meditation during the morning service. The earlier period was also useful because often there came to individuals illuminations of their own problems which made it unnecessary for them to seek any other help."

Thurman also used what he described as "creative silence" to engage in visits with the sick who remained behind after he had moved to a new place. He recounts the story of how he prayed with an ill woman living in another state by telling her that he would "meet her in the silence" twice a week, at an agreed-upon time. "Each time I came home for a brief visit, we would share our experiences.

Again and again we discovered that distance became more and more irrelevant. At last it seemed as if there was no distance separating us at all."

PRELUDE TO AN ENCOUNTER WITH GOD

Howard Thurman also believed that quieting the mind prepares us for an encounter with God. Solitude reduces the chance that interruptions and distractions will interfere. In the silence, an ineffable experience may occur, or we might simply hear some badly needed advice. Stillness, which we often experience outside in nature, provides a calming force. "Be still and know that I am God," the psalmist writes (Psalm 46:10). It is easier to connect with the presence of God or spiritual guidance when both inner and outer noises are minimized.

Arguing for the connection between regular meditation and encounters with God, Thurman writes, "Prayer is not only the participation in the communication with God in the encounter of religious experience, but is also the 'readying' of the spirit for such communication. It is the total process of quieting down and to that extent it must not be separated from meditation. Perhaps as important as prayer itself, is the 'readying' of the spirit for the experience."

Thurman later illustrates the importance of silence in *Disciplines of the Spirit*, observing that different kinds of silences fulfill a variety of purposes: "There is silence which is the prelude to prayer—the moment of hush and ingathering. There is a silence that tends to quiet the soundless words that fall from the tongue and to calm the noises of the mind and spirit. Every person who is concerned about the discipline of prayer must find the ministry of silence in accordance with his particular needs."

Observers have noted how important silence was to Howard Thurman. As Reverend Wayne B. Amason says, "Thurman specifically described the discipline and experience of the silence he practiced as a prelude to prayer. Yet throughout his writings, one comes away with the recognition that the active practice of silent meditation and contemplation was from his earliest years a deep well from which Thurman drew strength every day."

There is a difference between *feeling* the stillness that we experience outside in nature and *surrendering* to the stillness within. Quieting our hearts and minds is far more challenging than we might think. To observe the serenity of a hawk in flight, clouds drifting across the sky, or trees gently swaying in a breeze is to enter one kind of stillness. Being intentional about sitting down, closing our eyes, breathing deeply, and slowly decluttering our minds of all the racing thoughts: that is a different—and a more difficult—matter. In his lovely meditation "How Good to Center Down," Thurman says that "our minds seethe with endless traffic." But he knew that below the distracting chatter lies a deep reservoir of stillness—a place emanating with a peace that passes understanding and is filled with undeniable joy. Thurman also provides ideas about how to quiet the mind: "Perhaps an image of a quiet, still place, or reading one of the Psalms or a 'remembered radiance.'"

Going inward to connect with God generates an inner resolve. There we find strength to cope with the horrors of oppression or the pains and stresses of everyday life.

SILENCE MAY NOT BE FOR EVERYONE

When I was younger, the worst punishment my parents could mete out was to make my siblings and me go to our rooms with no television, radio, or books allowed. Even within the prison system, solitary confinement is one step below a death sentence. Silence is frequently used as a form of torture.

Silence has also been used to suppress entire groups, especially women and members of marginalized castes. People who have experienced being silenced feel negatively about silence itself. "Those who have been traumatized by oppression may be uncomfortable with reflective and meditative activities," writes theologian Barbara Holmes. "To survive, one must inevitably stow feelings, dysfunction, and myriad other 'healthy' responses to systematic abuse. Those who have buried these issues in the center of their souls are not anxious to participate in activities that will bring the memories and pain back to consciousness."

In addition, many people today actively avoid silence to the point of leaving electronic devices or the television on all day and night. Simply being alone without a smartphone, tablet, or computer feels, to them, like a severe penalty. When we attempt to quiet the outside as well as the inside chatter, unpleasant thoughts and feelings can arise. When I talk about the benefits of a silent retreat, many people shudder and say they could never do that, as the silence and solitude would feel too unsettling.

It may indeed be unwise for people who have recently suffered a trauma or experienced a great loss to sit regularly in silence. If something—a fear, oppression, an unnamed pain, or an unhealed wound—keeps one from silence, there are many other options for spiritual growth. Seeking professional assistance by meeting with a counselor or therapist could be helpful as well. Yet most of us can trust Howard Thurman's invitation to quiet time as a fitting opportunity to offer up the pain or hurt to "the love of God" for healing. Avoiding silence may prolong the pain and lead to stagnation. Barbara Holmes writes, "As frightening as it may be to 'center down,' we must find the stillness at the core of the shout, the pause in the middle of the 'amen,' as first steps toward restoration."

Howard Thurman inspires us to experience for ourselves why silence is golden, stillness is platinum, and solitude is transformative. He describes it best in this way:

> Once the interference that drowns out the hunger has been stilled or removed, real communion between man and God can begin. Slowly the hunger begins to stir until it moves inside the individual's self-consciousness, and the sense of the very Presence of God becomes manifest. The words that are uttered, if

there be words, may be halting and poor; they may have to do with some deep and searching need of which the individual now becomes acutely aware, it may be a sin that had become so much a part of the landscape of the soul, that the soul itself had the feeling of corruption—but this may not last long. On the other hand, it may be a rather swift outpouring of a concern, because here is the moment of complete understanding and the freedom it inspires.

REFLECTION QUESTIONS

- How would you describe your experiences with silence, stillness, and solitude?

- Reflect on your relationship with silence. Are you apprehensive or at ease? Are you friends, enemies, or occasional companions with silence?

- Have you ever thought about taking a weekend or longer for a silent retreat? Why or why not?

SPIRITUAL STEPS

- Try to take a day or half-day of solitude without distractions or noise—no television, podcasts, radio, music, or phone. Journal about how it feels to befriend quietness for a time.

- Take a few "pause pockets"—one, two, or three minutes of silence—throughout the day.

- Experiment with creative silence. For a month or two, invite one or two friends who live nearby or in another state or country to join you at exactly the same time (synchronizing time zones) each week for some silence. Gather periodically to discuss any insights, musings, or transformations.

CHAPTER 3

SIGNATURE OF GOD

EXPERIENCE NATURE AS THE DOORWAY TO THE DIVINE

*When I was a boy I was always driven to worship when I saw
a storm come up on the shores of the Atlantic Ocean on the
Florida coast. A stillness pervaded everything. The tall sea grass
stood at attention. As far out as my eye could go the surface of
the sea was untroubled, quiet, but expectant. I could almost
hear the pounding of my own heart against my ribs.*

—Howard Thurman, *Mysticism and Social Change*

Young Howard Thurman frequently rowed a small boat on
the Halifax River near his home in Daytona Beach, Florida,
and wandered the woods nearby. Nature became a place
for him to flee the physically and psychologically terroriz-
ing atmosphere of the Jim Crow South in the early 1900s.
Outdoors, he could momentarily escape this reality and sense
a oneness with everything: trees, the ocean, and the night sky.

As children, many of us discovered solace outside. Perhaps we felt attached to a loving and expansive Presence outside long before we ever felt God inside a church. Howard Thurman gives voice to the often inchoate sense of the sacred that children experience in the natural world. "The ocean and the night together surrounded my little life with a reassurance that could not be affronted by the behavior of human beings," he writes. "The ocean at night gave me a sense of timelessness, of existing beyond the reach of the ebb and flow of circumstances. . . . The experience of these storms gave me a certain overriding immunity against much of the pain with which I would have to deal in the years ahead when the ocean was only a memory. The sense held: I felt rooted in life, in nature, in existence."

Scholars often label Thurman a "nature mystic." Thurman would likely argue that an experience of God can happen anywhere: in nature, during worship, or while in private prayer. It is clear, however, that his awareness of his connection to God began outdoors. In his autobiography and several other books, Thurman mentions that something ineffable called him outside at an early age. He considered nature to be a friend, consoler, and source of mystical union:

> As a child I was accustomed to spend many hours alone in my rowboat, fishing along the river, when there was no sound save the lapping of the waves against the boat. These were times when it seemed as if the earth and river and the sky and I were one

beat of the same pulse. It was a time of watching and waiting for what I did not know—yet I always knew. There would come a moment when beyond the single pulse beat there was a sense of Presence which seemed always to speak to me. My response to the sense of Presence always had the quality of personal communion. There was no voice. There was no image. There was no vision. There was God.

In nature's quietness, Thurman could hear what he called "the harmony of creation." Nature represents the interrelatedness of all things. Through his writings, he reminds us how the divine dwells among us and is particularly palpable outside. As we walk with Howard Thurman through nature, we learn from his keen observations. We begin to read the symbols of the divine that populate outside spaces. "The signature of God is all around me," Thurman writes, "in the rocks, in the trees, in the minds of men." The sense of unity and rootedness he felt in nature transformed into overarching themes for his life and work.

THE PEACE OUTDOORS

Serenity, exhilaration, awe: these are common words people use for what they feel when they spend time outdoors. Awe, especially, triggered by beholding a spectacular waterfall, a rolling countryside, or a field of flowers, is a feeling we associate with the numinous. Visions and voices, indescribable peace, and fleeting moments of transcendence make nature a home for God, a place for spiritual awakenings or even conversions.

When I read about Thurman's experiences in nature, my heart leaped. I had not been the only Black child to uncover God outdoors! As a child, when I sat alone on the grass with my eyes closed, visiting relatives and neighbors with concerned faces would ask my mom and dad what I was doing. My sense was that wider culture's awareness of Black people's relationship with the natural world was limited as well. Absent from daily view were pictures of Black folks fishing, hiking, and camping. Thurman's description of his rendezvous with nature validated my own mystical leanings.

My desire to sit in the wind began at age four, when I discovered nature's deep peace. It was a tranquility nearly absent everywhere else—including church. The holy connection I felt when I was outdoors was devoid of the fear that lurked in my childhood image of God as an angry, punishing old white man. I didn't associate my longing to sit in the wind or my astonishment at nature's curiosities with God. As young children, Thurman and I both lacked the vocabulary to name such occurrences. My spiritual awareness expanded, but without language for what was happening. Much later, when I was older, I would read a scripture relating the Spirit to the wind: "The wind blows where it wishes and you hear the sound of it, but do not know where it comes from and where it is going; so is everyone who is born of the Spirit" (John 3:8).

I had not yet read about a nature-based custom common among the enslaved Gullah people, African Americans who lived along the coast of and on the islands near South Carolina. Gullah youth would go out into nature to find God in a spiritual coming-of-age ritual. In Gullah communities, the Praise House was a central fixture. To be baptized and assume full membership in the church and the community, a young candidate had to provide testimony in the Praise House about a spiritual experience they had. This time of preparation was called "seekin." Although the term is derived in part from Methodist missionaries who, after preaching and teaching, inquired if anyone wanted to "seek Jesus," the Gullah culture adapted the term to describe their own notion about potential believers. Margaret Creel, in her outstanding book on slave religion in Gullah culture, writes, "A candidate's acceptance into the church and subsequently into the Praise House depended upon relating a satisfactory experience, which was the result of a soul-grappling, traumatic confrontation between the individual and a higher power, culminating, if successful, in a sensation of rebirth and full membership in the religious community."

The "seekin" experience for the candidate included assuming a temporary ascetic character: withdrawing from social life and wearing ragged clothing; going into the wilderness for solitude, meditation, visions, and night vigils; and communicating only with their spiritual teacher. Many of these practices were similar to those found in West Africa at that time.

The purpose of the "seekin" time was to examine the commitment of the candidate for baptism. This ritual managed to transform individualistic behavior into a more communal orientation and also heightened a young person's sense of their own value. "While 'seekin' culminated in acceptance of socialization through church membership, the experience of itself was a private one and a desire to 'seek Jesus' was a slave's personal decision, although not devoid of community pressure," Margaret Creel writes. "The travel, the visions, and the solitude possibly represented a bondperson's inner reflection and recognition of 'self' as opposed to his or her treatment as a 'thing' by the master."

While I didn't call my experiences in nature "seekin," and it's doubtful that Thurman did either, what the Gullah knew—and what young Howard's early life illustrates—is that the wisdom of nature is available if we choose to notice it. Thurman saw all of nature as a reflection of God.

We can see recurring patterns within his writing about the natural world—aspects of creation to which he paid special attention and through which he identified the signature of God.

TREES

Trees served as a nurturing presence, relationship partner, teacher, and metaphor for Howard Thurman. We see this in his kinship with the old oak tree that nourished his soul: "I needed the strength of that tree, and, like it, I would hold my ground. . . . I cultivated a unique relationship with the tree. . . . I could sit, my back against the trunk, and feel the same peace that would come to me in my bed at night. I could reach down in the quiet places of my spirit, take out my bruises and my joys, unfold them, and talk about them. I could talk aloud to the oak tree and know that it understood."

Even as a child, Howard realized he must master the sturdiness and rootedness of the oak tree to survive as a free human spirit in a world hostile to people who looked like him. Eyeing the trees that grow in coastal climates, he notes they learn to "bend with the wind" to survive the violent storms that sometimes arise from the ocean. People, too, must learn how to both steel themselves and bow when life crises arise.

Thurman articulates in one meditation the importance of rooting oneself in proper soil. Fascinated by an article in *National Geographic* magazine about a set of trees growing without water in the Sahara Desert, he writes in *Deep Is the Hunger* about a scripture from Jeremiah that emphasizes the importance of planting deep roots in God rather than placing one's faith in people, power, and material possessions. In their quest for water, these trees send their roots deep into the earth, far enough down to meet subterranean rivers full of nutrients. The trees can flourish in the desert with hot temperatures and winds and without surface water. Thurman concludes that like these trees, we can be fed by the deep inner reserves of the Creator.

Thurman's sense that his old oak tree understood him—that it had a consciousness, of sorts, by which it could console and embrace him—is now verified by scientific research. Botanists tell us that trees communicate, especially with each other, through an intricate intertwined root system, chemicals, electrical impulses, and scent. If an animal begins to chew on their leaves, they can warn other trees of a threat nearby. They also emit certain pheromones to attract beneficial predators to eat bugs or insects that are damaging to them.

Remarkably, trees also form communities. "Mother trees" feed food and water to younger seedlings and protect them. In some areas, the children of older trees continue to feed the stumps of their parents to keep them alive. Trees know how essential each tree is to their livelihood, so they live as interdependent networks to care for each other. Planned forests, or those often planted for commercial purposes, demonstrate the effects of disruption. Researchers find that seedlings who lack parent trees to care for them don't live as long as trees who live in families, where nutrients and wisdom are passed from one generation to the next. I think Thurman would have been pleased to learn of this research, as he had intuited something similar. Trees remind us, as Thurman did, of the interconnectedness of everything.

The regenerative patterns of trees in forests illustrate that life continues to recreate itself, even when forest fires or human-induced disasters wipe it out. Thurman underscores the spirit of life is alive in everything, even in what appears dead. In his meditation on jack pine seeds in *Meditations of the Heart*, Thurman writes that a jack pine seed cannot be released from its cone unless the intense heat of a forest fire forces it out. Although the forest is scorched, gentle sprouts of the jack pine trees remain in the midst of the destruction. Thurman relates this miracle of growth out of disaster to what can arise from the devastations in a human life. He believed that the same aliveness contained in the jack pine seed resides in each of us. Life may be suddenly and permanently devastated by a tragic car accident, crippling war injury, or cancer diagnosis. The process of recovery often leads to a startling spiritual awakening. The ordeal makes us more certain of God, and we emerge transformed.

Growth and regeneration are lodged in Thurman's notion of "the growing edge." These words later became the title of one of his meditations, and then of an entire book. A vivacious presence, he claims, and an aliveness in nature reveal themselves in trees. He writes,

> There is inherent in the nature of life what I call "the growing edge." We see it in nature; always vitality seems to be nestling deep within the heart of a dying plant. A kind of oak tree comes to mind. You have seen it. The leaves turn yellow and die, but they stay on the tree all winter. The wind, the storm, the sleet, the snow—nothing is able to dislodge these dead leaves from the apparently dead branches. . . . Then there begins to be a stirring deep within the heart of the tree. . . . What wind, storm, hail, sleet, ice could not do during the long winter,

now comes to pass very quickly because of the vitality inherent in the tree.

SUNRISES AND SUNSETS

Sunrises and sunsets are nature's daily reminders of the divine presence. Thurman refers to our responses to sunrises over a canyon or sunsets over an ocean as "radical amazement."

> *We are most alive when we are brought face to face with the response of the deepest thing in us to the deepest thing in life. Consider the hackneyed illustration of the beautiful sunset! We see the sunset, we recognize the color, shape, and the general quality of the atmosphere—to these we respond. Then in the midst of all of this something else emerges—the sunset opens a door in us and to us, to another dimension, timeless in quality, that can be described only as ineffable, awe-inspiring—then we know radical amazement. This we know in prayer at its best and highest.*

In *With Head and Heart*, Thurman writes a moving account of seeing the radiant peak of Mount Everest at dawn while traveling in India. For him it was a moment of transcendence, a flash of limitlessness when boundaries and all else disappeared.

When I lived in Boulder, Colorado, many years ago, daybreak and dusk over the Rocky Mountains stunned me every time I caught a glimpse. Transfixed by the light, coupled with a wisp of blue sky and passing clouds, I realized that I was never alone, never without divine assistance. The presence of God inhabits the beauty of the sun's appearance and disappearance each day.

RIVERS

Howard Thurman's captivation with rivers and streams began with his time rowing along the Halifax River near his childhood home. As his spiritual awareness and intellectual acumen expanded, Thurman unwrapped the profundity in the meaning of rivers as revealed in the Negro spirituals. In his book *Deep River: An Interpretation of Negro Spirituals*, he plumbs the depths of the spiritual "Deep River" to offer insights on life and God. For Thurman, a river serves as a symbol for life and its vicissitudes. Life ebbs and flows like a river does: never in a straight line but with twists and turns, around and over rocks and occasionally over cliffs, forming a waterfall.

If we envision ourselves as a riverbank, always being molded by the river flow, we see that we, too, are being shaped. "I cannot escape. All experience is raw material that goes in the making of me," writes Thurman. "While my experiences shape myself ultimately, yet I am not my experiences. I am an experiencer—but without my particular experiences I would not be who I am. I am what I am at any particular moment by standing on the shoulders of an infinite series of yesterdays."

Rivers undergo times of drought and flooding. We, too, move through alternating periods of emptiness and overflow. After achieving a major goal, for example, we may feel empty or drained. Thurman advises that we ponder which resources can replenish and restore our spirits. Do we need to pray, play, exercise, listen to music or dance, or go on retreat? Then there are times of disastrous flooding. Our lives move along smoothly until a major crisis or emotional overload hits: the death of a family member, a life-threatening illness, or a job loss. "It is the flood time of the river," Thurman writes of these times. He then offers this profound image of God's role in both drought and flood: "The answer of the flood time is a greater opening *to* the sea. The answer to the drought of the river is a larger opening *from* the sea (e.g., connecting with God through prayer, meditation, creative arts). The sea is the answer both to the drought and the flood time of the river."

For Thurman, all waters come from the sea and return to it. "The goal and the source of the river are the same!" Like a river, life within us is seeking union with its Source. "The goal of the river is the sea . . . the river must answer the call of the sea. . . . Life is like that! The goal of life is God! The source of life is God!" Like rivers, we as human spirits remain unsettled until we find our way back to the sea, which is our Source.

CREATURES

Thurman believed that animals offer instruction about life and the divine Presence. He painted and collected replicas of penguins, and he was particularly intrigued with emperor penguins. Known to family and friends as a consummate storyteller, Thurman, eyes sparkling, would sometimes lean back in a chair and begin to laud emperor penguins, especially the males, for their adamant partnership. Emperor penguins represent teamwork, as both males and females work to ensure that their unhatched egg is protected. They exchange roles—to provide warmth and protection or gather food for their survival. Hence, their chicks are more likely to survive than the young of other penguin species. Thurman repeatedly cited this tale to emphasize the importance of working together and also as a metaphor about one's dreams. "It [a dream] must be sheltered and protected and kept close to the heart during all the cold, dark experiences of life until it hatches in the light of the sun."

My own interest in the collaborative efforts of bees echoes Thurman's intrigue with the penguins. I'm new to beekeeping, and my first colony consists of rescue bees: bees who choose to swarm or build colonies in inconvenient places like attics or on the sides of mailboxes and who are rescued rather than exterminated. I've observed how bees work together to support the colony. Each bee—queen, drones, and worker bees—holds a specific role. Bees are vital pollinators that sustain us. Without them, we could not produce fruits and vegetables, and human survival would be in jeopardy. Every meal we eat involves insects, flowering vegetation, farmers, farm workers, truckers, highway construction workers . . . and the list goes on.

"We are utterly dependent upon one another," Thurman writes. "We are the heirs of social experience, even for the very words we use. We are dependent upon one another for the food we eat, the clothes we wear. The sense of dependence is evident everywhere."

VISIONS

Contemplatives and mystics regularly report visions, which can occur anywhere but frequently happen when people are in nature. Harriet Tubman, Julian of Norwich, Hildegard of Bingen, Jesus: all experienced visions in nature. Visions were quite common for Howard Thurman as well. One day Thurman felt compelled to pray and while doing so received a vision of his older sister, Henrietta, suffering in bed. While he was praying, a telegram arrived from his mother directing him to come home immediately. By the time he arrived, Henrietta had died of typhoid fever. Thurman also recollects a "visitation" that occurred after the stabbing of Martin Luther King Jr. that moved him to visit King at once.

But the most consequential vision for Thurman was of a different sort, and it happened when he was outside. During his pilgrimage to India, he and his wife, Sue, visited the rugged, mountainous Khyber Pass on the border between Pakistan and Afghanistan.

> Near the end of our journey we spent a day in Khyber Pass on the border of the northwest frontier. It was an experience of vision. We stood looking at a distance

into Afghanistan, while to our right, and close at hand, passed a long camel train bringing goods and ideas to the bazaars of North India. . . . All that we had seen and felt in India seemed to be brought miraculously into focus. We saw clearly what we must do somehow when we returned to America. We knew that we must test whether a religious fellowship could be developed in America that was capable of cutting across all racial barriers, with a carry-over into the common life, a fellowship that would alter behavior patterns of those involved.

Among all of Thurman's foresight, this particular vision remained momentous. It represented his lifelong quest to promote community and to awaken in others a sense of unity and wholeness. This vision manifested in the church he cofounded and in his attempt to create a similar atmosphere at Marsh Chapel at Boston University. With his writing, Thurman would devote the remainder of his life to responding to this moment.

COMMON CONSCIOUSNESS

Howard Thurman felt that there was a knowingness—what he called "common consciousness"—that we could access in nature. We are connected to this common consciousness, yet our awareness of it may remain dormant or underdeveloped. This attunement with the divine may account for why animals often sense and respond to approaching natural disasters like earthquakes or tsunamis. "He remembered the day he had gone out before dawn to fish," his biographer writes of a time Thurman learned that the creaturely world tapped into this consciousness more than humans do. "A low bank of cloud often lay along the horizon and the sun would burn through it to light the land, but this day was different. . . . An hour later Howard was aware of a faraway roaring. It was not thunder. It was the bellowing of the giant 'gators in the distant freshwater swamps and it was a sign surer than any from the sky. The 'gators knew when a storm was coming."

In several sermons and writings, Thurman describes an event in his childhood as an illustration of common consciousness. One day as he approached a friend's house, he saw his friend's little sister, "less than a year old, sitting in the sand playing with a rattlesnake. It was an amazing and deeply frightening experience to watch. The child would turn the snake over on its side and do various things with him; the snake would crawl around her, then crawl back. It was apparent that they were playing together. . . . It was as if two different expressions of life, normally antagonistic to each, had dropped back into some common ground and there reestablished a sense of harmony through which they were relating to each other at a conscious level."

Common consciousness tethers all of creation to itself. We live in harmonious connection to trees, flowers, birds, and horses as well as other human spirits whether we are aware of it or not. Thurman considered the pursuit of this paradox—our personal consciousness as a river that fails to remember that it is a part of the ocean, of nature—to be his "working paper," or mission in life.

COMING ALIVE OUTSIDE

Thurman believed that we align ourselves with Life when we become aware of our common consciousness. The same Spirit that gives life to every living thing is the Source of our life as well.

Biographer Elizabeth Yates notes that Howard Thurman held unique ideas about nature for his time. Today he would likely be considered an environmentalist. Returning from India, he observed how Westerners viewed nature as an object to be conquered. "Nature was an enemy to be subdued and in the subduing the pioneer had developed a ruthless, destructive attitude," Yates writes. "He had not had the time yet to develop a oneness with woods and rivers and mountains which the Oriental [sic] had. There was a way to be found in which the Westerner could learn to affirm his community with the world around him and upon which he was totally dependent. 'Why does the forest speak its word to us?' Howard asked himself. 'It does, but we have been too busy to listen.'"

Thurman records a conversation with an Indigenous elder that illuminated for him the essential connections between nature and humans that he himself had intuited as a child:

> Man is a child of nature; he is rooted and grounded in the earth. He belongs to it, and it belongs to

him. I remember hearing an Indian chief from Northwestern Canada say: "I come from away up north near the Arctic Circle. I am a part of the snow, ice, and wind in the winter. These flow into me and I flow into them." Man cannot long separate himself from nature without withering as a cut rose in a vase. One of the deceptive aspects of mind in man is to give him the illusion of being distinct from and over against but not a part of nature. It is but a single leap thus to regard nature as being so completely other than himself that he may exploit it, plunder it, and rape it with impunity.

Diversity is written into nature, and that includes humanity itself. The natural world contributed to the absolute clarity of Thurman's conviction that segregation and discrimination of any kind are unnatural. Such human-imposed divisions are a denial of God, who is the Creator and Author of all life.

Thurman leaves us with this message: nature is a balm for the soul that seeks reconciliation and wholeness. Seeing manifestations of sacred unity everywhere is a powerful gift we can receive whenever we go outside.

REFLECTION QUESTIONS

- What spiritual gifts or lessons does nature offer you?
- What elements of nature spark awe within you? Have you had any transcendent experiences or moments of oneness outdoors?

- During turbulent and unsettling times, where do you seek solace? How does communing with nature comfort your spirit and calm your mind?

- Do you feel a part of nature? How do you work to be in harmony with it?

SPIRITUAL STEPS

- Sometimes we are so busy that we miss trees, birds, insects, stillness, or the sky speaking to us. Go outdoors and spend a few minutes noticing what is around you. Find one thing to focus on, whether it's a cloud, ant, bee, wind, tree, or flower. Pay attention to the details. Try not to analyze; just notice. What spiritual gifts does this moment offer you?

- Locate your favorite spot outside—a place where you come alive, if only for a few moments. What about this place shifts your attention or feels healing to you? What exactly do you feel—"radical amazement," peace, companionship, connection? Set up a recurring appointment with yourself to spend more time there.

- Take a walk or hike with a child. Look at nature through their eyes. Sit in the backyard with an elderly relative or neighbor. Notice how you feel when you begin and when you finish.

- Take an imaginary walk or hike. Where would you go—a park, a beach, mountains, a forest, a neighborhood? What do you notice during your imaginary walk? What season have you chosen to walk in? How might your choices reveal how you connect with the divine when you are outdoors?

CHAPTER 4

THE GENUINE IN YOU

RECOGNIZE EVERYONE AS A HOLY CHILD OF GOD

Whatever may be the occasion there comes a deep necessity which leads you finally into the closet with yourself. It is here that you raise the real questions about yourself. The leading one is, What is it, after all, that I amount to, ultimately? Such a question cuts through all that is superficial and trivial in life to the very nerve center of yourself. And this is a religious question because it deals with the total meaning of life at its heart. . . . The most crucial clue to a knowledge of [God] is to be found in the most honest and most total knowledge of the self.

—Howard Thurman, *The Inward Journey*

One night in 1910, Howard Thurman's mother woke him up and coaxed him outside. She wanted him to catch a glimpse of Halley's Comet, which is only visible from Earth about every seventy-five years. Thurman's father had died a few years earlier. Looking up at the comet blazing against the Florida sky that night, young Howard asked his mother what would happen if the comet fell to Earth. She looked at Howard with great serenity. He need not worry, his mother told him, because God would take care of them.

This experience stayed with Thurman his entire life. "It was not until my experience with Halley's Comet that there began to emerge a faint but growing sense of personal destiny, religious in tone and spiritual in accent," he writes in his autobiography. Ever since, he claims, "I have never been totally cut off from a sense of the guidance of my life. . . . It was more than mere ego-affirmation, as important as it is—it was a clue to my self-worth in the profoundest sense. It was the shield against the denigration of my environment; but much, much more."

Howard Thurman narrates this same event in *Jesus and the Disinherited*: "The majestic power of my mother's glowing words has come back again and again, beating out its rhythmic chant in my own spirit," he writes. "Here are the faith and the awareness that overcome fear and transform it into the power to strive, to achieve, and not to yield." Without intending to describe a psychological phenomenon, Howard Thurman points to the way that anchoring ourselves in God leads to high levels of self-esteem and self-efficacy. As he notes, a formidable faith and assurance spring from the conviction that "I am a holy child of God." It exudes a reliance on God's guidance and protection. Marcus Borg would later describe this same stance espoused by Jesus as not a mere belief in God but, rather, a radical trust in God.

As I closed my heavily underlined copy of Thurman's autobiography, I kept thinking of that moment between a young Howard and his mother, the way she used a child's question to strengthen his sense of being God's beloved child. That scene illumines so much. Howard Thurman wanted people to see themselves as creations of God and to convey that same awareness to children. This certainty—that he was a holy child of God—anchored and guided Thurman. He understood that knowing, believing, internalizing, and acting from a divine center transform all of life. How could he spark this wisdom in other denigrated human spirits—Black people in America who yearned to know and express their authentic selves?

Thurman garnered immense personal strength from defining himself based on his spirit, his inner self, rather than by attributes projected onto him by society. Understanding what it meant to be a holy child of God—to possess a spiritual self—he discovered its link to self-esteem, achievement, and self-actualization. In one recorded conversation, Thurman describes it in this way: "It goes back to my childhood, because I had constantly to affirm my own self in an environment that reduced me to zero, an environment in which I had no standing, as it were. I was driven to find in the grounds of my being that which transcended everything in my environment (external to me). Once I hit it, then I knew I was home free, that the environment could never destroy me because at my center I would never say 'yes' to the external judgment of me [as a Black man]."

Introducing children to the notion that they are holy children of God is vital, especially for children in communities that have been marginalized and dispossessed. The sense of being a holy child of God both centers the Creator as the primary source of identity and grounds the self in God. Nancy Ambrose, Howard Thurman's grandmother, knew she was a holy child of God, and this recognition enabled her to survive the ravages of slavery. As she witnessed the light and joy in the eyes of her grandchildren fade as they grew older, she became determined to convey this insight to them. Grandma Nancy saw the erosion of their confidence and sense of worthiness as their awareness of their second-class citizenship in the segregated Jim Crow South sank into their consciousness.

Thurman often recounted a tale his grandmother told to him and his two sisters. She would tell them how once or twice a year the slave master permitted a slave preacher to preach to the slaves. After he finished his sermon, he would look each slave in the eye and tell all of them, "You are not niggers! You are not slaves! You are God's children." When she finished, Thurman's and his sisters' spirits felt revived.

Luther Smith Jr., in his wonderful book *Howard Thurman: Mystic as Prophet*, writes, "Nancy Ambrose was the first to teach Thurman that spirituality sustains one in the midst of life's many predicaments. . . . She witnessed to the power of her spirituality to meet one of the fundamental demands of life's hierarchy of needs: the need to survive as a slave. This survival function of religion is not just addressing the condition of the body, but the survival of an identity—that center of a person which gives definition to one's being."

Thus, from an early age, Thurman learned from his grandmother's and mother's examples, which included regular religious practices such as prayer, Bible reading, church attendance, and spiritual conversations. Through their stories and modeling, young Howard became partially inoculated against the oppressive, racist messages surrounding him.

SPIRITUALITY THAT GETS PASSED DOWN

When caregivers are conscious of their innate connection to God, they transmit a certain confidence to children. They inspire hope and high achievement rather than despondency and despair. Thurman notes, "I have seen it happen in communities that were completely barren, with no apparent growing edge, without any point to provide light for the disadvantaged, I have seen children grow up without fear, with quiet dignity and such high purpose that the mark which they set for themselves has even been transcended." When children experience an unconditionally loving relationship with caregivers, they may assume that God loves them too. For a child, parental love and God's love speak the same language.

I think of the nuns in my parochial school, who constantly reminded me and my classmates that we were God's holy children and that we should speak and act accordingly. Being a holy child of God made me feel special, confident, and smart. Like Thurman, I had unknowingly discovered and begun to cultivate an unseen, transcendent, and powerful aspect of myself—a spiritual self.

Not everyone has a loving family and community. The converse of unconditional love can undermine children's relationships with themselves and God. Parents, grandparents, caregivers, or teachers who do not realize they are holy children of God may unintentionally communicate a sense of limitation and restriction to children. "The doom of the children is the greatest tragedy of the disinherited," writes Thurman. "They are robbed of much of the careless rapture and spontaneous joy of merely being alive. So many tender, joyous things in them are nipped and killed without their even knowing the true nature of their loss. The normal for them is abnormal." Lack of a loving relationship with a parent or caregiver in childhood may result in emotional and spiritual inhibitions and extend into adulthood.

REVERENCE FOR THE SELF

As I read more about Thurman's perspectives, I ran into his work on the sanctity of the self. Thurman thought deeply about his own childhood and later about the religious philosophies introduced to him in seminary. In his writing, he makes two assertions about the development of an *accurate* sense of self. First, each of us is inherently worthy because God created us. We may not feel worthy when we do not receive positive messages about ourselves from our families and the larger world. For Thurman, self-image must be congruent with this idea of intrinsic worthiness. Otherwise, our self-esteem becomes distorted by the lack of affirmation from parents, peers, and teachers. You may question your worthiness if you enter a store and a shop owner follows you around because they assume people who look like you are likely to steal. Lost are the strength, self-determination, and direction that come from living with a *true* sense of self.

Thurman's next declaration about an accurate sense of self involves belonging. In many ways, our self-definition arises out of relationships, and our stability is dependent on them. He writes,

> *In order to answer the questions, "Who am I?" the individual must go on to ask, "To whom, to what do I belong?" This primary sense of belonging, of counting, of participating in situations, of sharing with the group, is the basis of all personal stability. And from it is derived the true sense of self. We are all related either positively or negatively to some immediate social unit which provides the other-than-self reference which in turn undergirds the sense of self. Such a primary group confers persona upon the individual; it fashions and fortifies the character structure. It is so important that most of our choices, decisions and actions are taken in the light of their bearing upon relationship with the group or groups that give to us dignity, self-respect, status, a sense of self.*

In Thurman's view, the sanctity of the self is essential. Jesus modeled this notion by affirming every person. Poor Jews, women, Samaritans, Roman soldiers, lepers, tax collectors: all are created by God and thus innately deserving. Once we ground ourselves in this realization, we are better able to assess our own potential. Howard Thurman describes it plainly: "The psychological effect on the individual of the conviction that he is a child of God gives a note of integrity to whatever he does." People like his grandmother, who centered her life in God, exuded a quiet dignity, a certain holiness that she infused into her work as a laundress and midwife. For the dispossessed, this shift in self-definition helps to illuminate the discriminatory treatment they receive. Unfair practices and injustices result not from their lack of worth or intelligence but from the actions of individuals who wish to restrict their freedom and growth. This liberating sentiment is key to understanding Howard Thurman's life and work.

In psychology classes that I taught, I tried to help students dissect the connections between self-concept and other identities like gender, race, ethnicity, and religion. As infants, we arrive in the world without knowing anything about gender, ethnicity, race, or what these labels mean. An initial sense of self emerges from what other individuals and groups convey to us about who we are. But are these meanings true and accurate? How can one of God's creations be less holy than another because of their phenotype, culture, or religion? As we walk with Thurman, here is a moment when he might ask us to pause, take a seat on a bench, and ponder.

The awareness that one is a holy child of God doesn't appear out of nowhere but is nurtured over time. So is there a spiritual self, or is spirituality only one facet of the self? How does self-concept originate? And can it change as we mature and grow?

SELF OR SPIRITUAL SELF?

My students often found the most intriguing part of a course on self-concept to be the idea of a spiritual self, as proposed by psychologist William James. Buried beneath all the imposed identities (race, gender, social status) and acquired identities (parent, musician, athlete, scientist) is a spiritual self, waiting to be uncovered. The concept of a spiritual self offers another lens through which to view Thurman's ideas about the self and its link to spirituality.

In many ways the question "Who are you?" is an inquiry about both the self and our personal relationship with God. Thurman suggests that within the answer lies a description of our spiritual condition, the degree to which we are conscious of our spiritual self. Where do we go for help, and where does the courage come from that allows us to be who we truly are? If you know for certain you are a holy child of God, you will seek the presence of God within. God will provide the strength to be your unique self and to actualize your potential. The fear about taking risks—to move to a new city, start a new job, or work for social justice—lessens.

Thurman scholar Mozella Mitchell notes that Howard Thurman and Carl Jung held similar notions of the self: that the self is the essence and the ego an overlay. The self is what we offer to God. In one meditation, "The Many Selves Become One," Thurman discusses the possibility that there may be "many divisions within the inner circle of the Self. When we enter into communion with Him we are never sure of the true Voice that speaks within us." Mitchell summarizes the connection between self and God in Thurman's work:

> Thurman pictures various voices as the sound of some past desire unfilled, an echo of some impulse to good we have pushed aside in favor of a more personal goal, the call of some common everyday need. Describing the Voice as sometimes a clarion call rising above the conflicting voices and at other times a muted sound, he says that all the time we pull back from the Voice because the other voices detain us. The true Voice is the true self that must emerge from far beneath all the other noises (voices); it is emerging from the unconscious, seemingly. . . . The true self, then, is God deep within the self responding to God beyond the self. It is what Jung terms the "spirit." It is the psyche. . . . It is not certain that Thurman would agree fully with this analysis of spirit, but his connection of the self with spirit and psyche is similarly achieved.

SPIRITUAL SELF AND HIGH SELF-ESTEEM

In *Jesus and the Disinherited*, Howard Thurman poses the question that recurs specifically for the disinherited: "Who am I?" Many cues about the self emerge not only from family and friends but from the larger society. Those who are marginalized can begin to believe their lives do not matter. Thurman, however, felt a person could possess personal worth but still feel inhibited by a sense of social inferiority if not allowed to participate fully in society. He writes, "The awareness of being a child of God tends to stabilize the ego and results in a new courage, fearlessness, and power. I have seen it happen again and again." The feeling of being connected to something transcendent—which he often labeled "the Eternal"—helps to immunize the disinherited from the fear that accompanies the violence and aggression they regularly witness.

For Thurman, religion can assure each individual of their birthright as a child of God. With God as the basis for self-esteem, a person gains a sense of wholeness and an inner life that is not regulated by the outside environment. Thurman states, "Often there are things on the horizon that point logically to a transformation of society, especially for the underprivileged, but he cannot co-operate with them because he is spiritually and intellectually confused. He mistakes fear for caution and caution for fear. Now, if his mind is free and his spirit unchained, he can work intelligently and courageously for a new day. Yes, with calmness and relaxation, as sons of God, the underprivileged may fling their defiance into the teeth of circumstances as they work out their salvation with fear and trembling as to God."

To suggest that claiming our spiritual selves assures we will live a life of courage and triumph is far too simplistic. Being aware of myself as a holy child of God or a spiritual self does not mean I won't question myself when I suffer a microaggression or outright discrimination. But a sense of inner authority, a topic I will address later, is awakened when we learn we are a holy child of God.

THE NEED FOR SELF-REFLECTION

Disentangling what we are told about ourselves from what resonates inside of us requires ongoing self-reflection. "Women without children are abnormal." "Black people aren't smart enough to complete graduate school." "I wouldn't live in *that* neighborhood." These are but a few of the many external voices I have heard throughout my life. But did any of these directives mirror my inner life or the Inner Guidance I received?

The recognition that we are holy children of God may arrive in many different ways. Encountering the divine in nature or through a particular song may awaken a slumbering spiritual self. Through illness, the loss of a loved one, or a treasured occupation, we may learn to know ourselves in new ways. We may stumble upon our spiritual selves in therapy or spiritual direction, or in conversations with a friend, or on retreat. "Stripped to the literal substance of ourselves, what is it that we want and need in order to be worthful persons in our own sight?" Howard Thurman asks.

When we pose piercing questions about our self and our crucial relationships, we begin to uncover a self freed of all the obligations or "shoulds." Taking time to engage in self-reflection moves us toward our true, authentic self.

DEVELOPING AND NURTURING A SPIRITUAL IDENTITY

The spiritual self expands and matures when we attend to what it yearns for. We must nourish our spiritual selves just like we feed our bodies. The spiritual self seeks community, and so many of us flourish in a congregation, in a choir, or in liturgical or religious rituals. For others, reading from sacred texts or the work of wisdom figures, invoking quiet listening, or practicing yoga or tai chi feeds the spiritual yearning. Some spiritual selves search for oneness in the stillness and vastness of nature. Gardening, fishing, sewing, knitting, and dancing easily connect us to the transcendent nature of God. Painting, playing an instrument, or losing ourselves in a character on stage can create an unbridled joy. A brisk walk or run each day may add a spark to the spiritual self. Being present to these activities can quiet the ego chatter of the mind and allow space for the spiritual self to be heard.

Howard Thurman would be delighted, I think, to see all the contemporary expressions of spirituality integrated into the common life. He would remind us that knowing we are holy children of God creates a kind of intimacy with God, which provides us with guidance, strength, a sense of being cared for, and a sense of purpose. He would urge us to live from an authentic or a spiritual self, the divine center that gives way to coming alive.

UNINTENDED CONSEQUENCES

The understanding that I am a holy child of God contains within itself often unrealized consequences. If I embrace this notion about myself, I must accept its corollary: that is, if I am a holy child of God, then so *is everyone else*. This sentiment is echoed in an interview in which Howard's daughter, Olive Thurman Wong, bemoaned the fact that people didn't fully comprehend the importance of oneness in her father's life and work. "'Oneness' is an easy enough thing to bandy about," writes Thurman scholar Liza Rankow, who interviewed Wong. "It is even an easy thing to profess, until we realize that it must include not only the people we like and agree with, not only those to whom we are sympathetic, but also those whom we view as abhorrent (whatever side of a political position we may hold). We don't get to choose who we are one with—it's everybody."

Sometimes the faces of the people I detest flash across my mind and heart: people who espouse hatred and harm others, people whose political, economic, or theological opinions I find unacceptable. How can they possibly be holy children of God? Howard Thurman answers this question in the final chapter of *Jesus and the Disinherited*. Pointing to the centrality of the love ethic in Jesus's teachings, he observes the types of people Jesus befriended who, by all accounts, should have been absolute enemies. Thurman points to the necessity of extinguishing bitterness within the heart in order to recognize adversaries as holy children of God.

In the Gospels, Thurman suggests, Jesus issues an even greater challenge: "Jesus demonstrated that the only way to redeem them for the common cause was to penetrate their thick resistance to public opinion and esteem and lay bare the simple heart," writes Thurman. "This man is not just a tax collector; he is a son of God. Awaken that awareness in him and he will attack his betrayal as only he can—from the inside. It was out of this struggle and triumph that Jesus says to love and do good for those who persecute you. Likewise, the same must be applied to those who represent the oppressive state. To love the Roman meant first to lift him out of the general classification of enemy."

Howard Thurman knew that we need to perceive enemies and oppressors as people stripped of any privileges so that they can treat each other as holy children of God. This position speaks to his own ongoing belief in the unity of all human spirits regardless of their position in life.

How do you know you are living as a holy child of God? How do you live from your spiritual self? "There is something in every one of you that waits, listens for the genuine in yourself," Thurman said in one of his last public lectures, a baccalaureate address to the students of Spelman College. "You are the only you that has ever lived; your idiom is the only idiom of its kind in all existences, and if you cannot hear the sound of the genuine in you, you will all of your life spend your days on the ends of the strings that somebody else pulls."

REFLECTION QUESTIONS

- What did you learn as a child about your spiritual life?

- Do you feel more than one self coexisting within you? When are you most likely to feel your spiritual self— outside, during a worship service, early in the mornings, or when reading inspirational material? How does being aware of your spiritual self enhance your connection with others?

- Which of your selves, or identities, seems most prominent in your life? Which self directs your thoughts, feelings, and actions? Do you feel freed by this self or captive to it?

SPIRITUAL STEPS

- Make a list of the attributes or characteristics or skills that come naturally to you. Maybe it's your love of nature, or cooking, or singing, or composing music. Spend some time today connecting with your spiritual self by doing one or more of the things you listed.

- Do you know someone who seems to live from a spiritual self, out of an awareness of being a holy child of God? Arrange a conversation and listen to them about the steps it took.

CHAPTER 5

SACRED SYNCHRONICITY

PAY ATTENTION TO DIVINE INTERVENTION

*Again and again, we are reminded by the facts of our own
lives that there is an aspect of our experience which seems to
be beyond our own control and yet it seems ever to manipulate
us into position. When such things happen, we call them the
work of Fate or Destiny, or some other term which expresses
our ignorance of what is at work. The most convenient term
is coincidence. But this labeling does not indicate that we had
to find any terms; we have merely described a situation or a
result. . . . Coincidence—Fate—Providence—Chance—or the
Purpose of God?*

—Howard Thurman, *Meditations of the Heart*

Young Howard Thurman tossed aside financial and racial
obstacles to obtaining a secondary education and moved
beyond the oppressive atmosphere of Daytona Beach. At
the time, colored children were only permitted to complete
the seventh grade, thereby disqualifying them from a high

school education, which required eight years of formal classroom learning. But the Black community surrounding him came together to ensure that Thurman's keen intellect would have room to grow. The principal of his school personally tutored him through his eighth-grade studies and prepared him for the eighth-grade exam. Thurman agreed to work a number of jobs and arranged to stay with cousins in Jacksonville, Florida, so that he could attend Florida Baptist Academy.

Finally, the day young Howard was to board the train to Jacksonville arrived. At the station, he found that his one trunk, strapped together with rope, did not meet railroad regulations for his type of ticket. The trunk would have to be shipped separately, the railroad official informed him, and it would cost three dollars. Howard only had one dollar in his pocket. He sat down and cried. Then Howard heard a deep baritone voice asking him what was wrong. He opened his eyes and saw a large Black man in overalls, work boots, and a large denim cap. Thurman explained that he wanted to travel to Jacksonville so he could obtain a high school education but that he didn't have enough money to ship his trunk. The man signaled to Thurman to get up and follow him to the ticket office.

This complete stranger paid the remainder of the shipping cost for the trunk so Thurman could leave for high school. Years later, Thurman would dedicate his autobiography to the stranger who helped him. The memory of this moment of divine grace would also motivate him to establish the Howard Thurman Educational Trust. The trust created a scholarship program for students like Thurman so they could gain an education that would lift them out of poverty.

Has a person ever suddenly appeared with exactly what you need? Has a chance encounter or what seemed like happenstance changed your life? Have you ever opened a book to a phrase or word that solves a problem or illuminates what has been obscure? Are crazy coincidences just that—coincidence—or are they proof of God's intervention?

Walking my own spiritual path, filled with several holy coincidences of its own, I began to suspect that Howard Thurman's life would help me answer this question. From an early age, Thurman recognized that he was not the guide of his life but an inquisitive explorer on an extraordinary expedition. He frequently felt himself to be the beneficiary of "uncanny coincidences" or "providential accidents." As he reflected on his life, Thurman found it full of the presence and power of God. He also engaged the Creator by yielding many decisions in prayer, waiting and listening for a "word in my heart."

Many Christians see God's hand in everything that happens, saying, "It's a God thing," or calling something a "God-wink." Many of us find it easy to dismiss what they call divine assistance or intervention as simply serendipity or chance. Thurman's views on divine intervention, however, offer a way out of simplistic claims that God ordains everything, on the one hand, or that everything happens by chance, on the other hand. Peter Eisenstadt, renowned Thurman scholar and biographer, ties the synchronistic occurrence at the train station to Thurman's notion of God. "Providence would be perhaps too strong a term for Thurman's belief, luck too weak. It was one of those uncanny linkages between two events, a brief moment when a hidden, benign undergirding and connectedness of the universe is glimpsed. If Thurman's God was in a live oak tree, God could also be found in a railway station." There would be other moments in Thurman's life, too, when an unexpected turn of events heralded a divine Presence. How might his life provide a lens through which to see the Holy working in our own?

GUARDIAN ANGEL

I cannot remember anyone appearing in such a compelling way to me as the man at the train station appeared to Thurman. Yet I experienced an unusual incident during my first trip out of the country. Years ago I had chosen to attend a fall conference in London on nonverbal communication, but I needed to have open-heart surgery in July. After the surgery and some basic recovery, I informed my cardiologist about the conference. He expressed extreme trepidation about traveling so soon after heart surgery. Then he handed me a list of cardiologists who practiced in London "just in case you run into trouble."

During an initial conference gathering, a tall German scholar in his mid-thirties, Klaus, sat next to me. As we chatted, I happened to mention my recent heart surgery, and he looked very concerned. The next day, Klaus met me at my door for breakfast, and from that point on, for the rest of my stay, he acted as a guardian angel. He gave me a slow walking tour of London, pointing out historical sights and hailing a taxi at one point because he thought I had over-exerted myself. One afternoon I had an extended attack of arrhythmia, or irregular heartbeats. Klaus was ready to call an ambulance, although the episode stopped after about two minutes. After my return to the United States, I wrote him a note of thanks, but I never saw or heard from him again. He had made it his primary assignment to make certain I lived through the seven-day conference. I sometimes wonder what he intuited about my precarious health that even I did not.

If I could share this story with Howard Thurman, I think he would affirm the belief that God sends guardian angels in the forms of strangers during times of our greatest need. After Thurman's first year at Florida Baptist Academy, he returned home malnourished and emaciated. At school he was eating only one meal per day and working and studying nonstop. Seeing his haggard appearance, his mother refused to allow him to stay off campus the next year. She wanted him to be looked after and cared for by adults.

Thurman could not imagine how he could afford room and board, so during that summer he furiously toiled at many odd jobs even though he knew he couldn't earn enough money. One day as he substituted for a friend at a shoeshine stand, he looked up at the gable on a house across the river, which happened to be the winter home of James Gamble, a founder of the Procter & Gamble Company.

Thurman felt an urge to write Gamble and ask for a loan. As he began writing a letter, he realized the impossibility of his venture: he didn't want anyone to know the nature of his request, nor did he know Gamble's address in Cincinnati, where he lived most of the year except for winters.

As Thurman rode his bicycle back to the shoeshine stand after a lunchbreak, a white woman waved him down. She said he looked trustworthy and ordered him to mail some letters. One of the letters was addressed to James Gamble! Thurman wrote down the address from the envelope and then sent his own letter to him. Gamble would end up supporting Thurman with a partial scholarship through the remainder of high school. This holy coincidence served as another answer to his prayer to God to continue his education.

Holy coincidences are not always pleasant. As we saw in the first chapter, the sermon at Howard's father's funeral traumatized him. Initially, he swore that when he became an adult, he would have nothing to do with the church. But he couldn't shake the way the ocean, the woods, and the old oak tree led him to a deep inner sense of the presence of God. He once said, "When I was born God must have put a live coal in my heart, for I was his man and there was no escape." Home for a visit from college one summer, Thurman accidentally encountered a preacher in town. When Thurman saw the man, he felt ill, but he did not know why. Later, as he described the man to his grandmother, she told him who it was. It was Sam Cromarte, the visiting clergyman who had condemned his deceased father to hell during his funeral. Thurman had been so young when his father died that he hadn't recognized him.

Somehow this incident gave Thurman a release from the unfounded belief that if he became a minister, he would betray his father. What had bolstered his ambivalence were Christian doctrines that dictated church membership as requisite for salvation and that allowed for segregated churches. These ideas seemed incongruent with the God he knew—the One who created and loved everyone: members and nonmembers, Christians and non-Christians. After that incident, he felt free to move toward what God had been calling him to for years.

SACRED SYNCHRONICITIES

God's timing appears impeccable. Sometimes a holy coincidence is a word or phrase on a billboard, in a book, or in the lyrics of a song that resonate deeply with something we've been thinking. On occasion we meet a person who acts like a "transitional object," or transfer agent; they cannot help us directly, but they connect us with another person who addresses our problem.

A momentous synchronicity occurred during Thurman's first church assignment in Oberlin, Ohio. One evening Thurman attended a conference on religious education in a nearby town. Becoming bored, he decided to step outside for some fresh air. On his way out, he passed a table with books for sale for ten cents each. He bought two, one of which had a very intriguing title—*Finding the Trail of Life*.

Right then and there, he sat down and read the book in its entirety. During his reading, he felt the author was speaking to him and describing his experiences as a young boy. He longed to meet and study with its author, Quaker mystic Rufus Jones. As soon as he returned home, he acquired as much information as he could about Jones, a distinguished professor of religion and mysticism at Haverford College, outside Philadelphia. He suspected that the college did not admit Negro students, but that did not prevent him from pursuing the possibility.

Meanwhile, Thurman was invited to present a worship experience for students at the University of Pennsylvania, in Philadelphia. While there, Thurman met his first Quaker, a gentleman who invited him to a winter meeting of Quakers. During the gathering, Thurman shared with this man how much he yearned to study mysticism with Rufus Jones. By happenstance—or holy coincidence?—the Quaker man shared that he had been friends with Rufus Jones for forty years and had even been his neighbor for some of that time. He agreed to talk with Jones on Thurman's behalf, and soon thereafter, Rufus Jones contacted Thurman for more details.

Jones provided Thurman, admitted as a special student, with graduate housing and no charge for tuition. Despite Thurman's recent appointment as a professor of religion and director of spiritual life at Morehouse/Spelman Colleges, he was able to secure a semester leave and the financial resources to support his family while studying with Jones at Haverford.

Through sacred synchronicities, Thurman had been led to a distinguished scholar of religion and mysticism. Later Thurman wove the knowledge he gained from Jones and his vast library on mysticism into meditations, sermons, and other writings. Once again, it seems, divine assistance supported Thurman's desire to pursue, in his own words, "that which moves with the grain in my own wood."

This story, along with several others from Thurman's life, reminds me of the neologism *pronoia*, which is the opposite of *paranoia*. While paranoia is the sense that others are out to do us harm, pronoia is the feeling that a force or divine presence is conspiring to help us. Howard Thurman could have likely filled an entire book with stories from his life that illustrate pronoia and implicate the workings of God. His history-making intersections with two leaders of nonviolent movements for human rights in the twentieth century may suggest something akin to divine coordination.

MAHATMA GANDHI

In October 1935, Thurman left on the pilgrimage to India. Prior to his trip he exchanged correspondence with Mahatma Gandhi. Gandhi knew the delegation's arrival and departure dates, and a telegram from him awaited their disembarkation in Colombo, Ceylon, saying he was eager to meet. But several attempts to connect with Gandhi throughout their six-month visit failed. First, Gandhi was sick. Then members of Thurman's delegation fell ill or suffered exhaustion from the demanding schedule. A foreboding began to arise in Thurman's spirit about whether the meeting would actually occur. Communication across distances was difficult, and planning a meeting was exceedingly more challenging than it is today. How would they find each other and a time to meet?

Finally in late February 1936, shortly before their scheduled egress, a divine episode occurred. Thurman shared it in his autobiography, and other biographers mention it quite frequently. Here is Peter Eisenstadt and Quinton Dixie's account:

> According to his autobiography on their second day in Bombay, as Thurman was going to the post office to telegraph to see if a meeting could be arranged, he spied a man with a Gandhi cap. "Our eyes met as we passed, though we said nothing. When I had gone about fifty feet something just made me turn around to look back at him just as he turned around to look back at me. He smiled; I smiled. We turned and came toward each other and when we met he said, 'Are you, you?' And I said, 'Yes.' He said, 'Well I have a letter for you from Gandhiji.'" It was another of the providential accidents that throughout his life Thurman found pregnant with deeper significance.

At three in the morning on February 21, 1936, after a three-and-a-half-hour train trip, Thurman, his wife, Sue, and Edward Carroll arrived at Gandhi's camp. Phenola Carroll had contracted scarlet fever and remained in Bombay. Exhausted, Sue and Edward took time to rest and joined the gathering later. Thurman went directly to meet with Gandhi because given the train schedule back to Bombay, they would have only a little more than three hours for their exchange.

In this historic conversation with Gandhi, Thurman gathered several insights. The discussion seemed filled with one epiphany after another and illuminated some notions Thurman wanted to explore. Oppression robs people of their self-respect and moral self-awareness, Gandhi shared, while unmerited violence disorganizes individuals from within. Legally sanctioned brutality might account for why oppressed people violate other oppressed people.

Gandhi and Thurman also discussed at length the concept of *ahimsa*—described by Gandhi as "a force superior to all the forces put together" and a force superior to brutality. This force—and there are really no words to describe it—underlies and defines all of reality. It is the ultimate force of love. Gandhi's philosophy seemed to gel with Thurman's ideas that there is "some underlying moral order to the universe" and that "The cosmos is the kind of order that sustains and supports the demands that the relationships between men and between man and God be one of harmony and integration."

Thurman ended up incorporating many of the ideas from this conversation into the book *Jesus and the Disinherited*. It's hard to overstate the importance of that meeting between Thurman and Gandhi—which almost didn't happen. Given the challenge that Gandhi issued to Thurman, who returned to share ideas with civil rights leaders in the United States, one wonders: how might the course of American history have changed had Thurman not crossed paths with a member of Gandhi's party that day?

MARTIN LUTHER KING JR.

After he and Sue returned from India in April 1936, they visited Atlanta. While there, they had dinner with their old friends the Kings: Martin Luther Sr. and Alberta. Sue and Alberta had been roommates at the then-residential Spelman High School. Consequently, Alberta, mother of Martin Luther King Jr., knew Sue Bailey Thurman before Martin Luther King Jr. was born. Historians and biographers are not sure whether Martin Jr., who would have been about seven years old at the time of the Thurmans' visit, participated in their evening together.

Martin Luther King Jr.'s parents shared in the Thurmans' excitement about what they had experienced in India, especially their intense discussion with Gandhi about nonviolence and civil disobedience. Later, when Thurman shared this story with historian, friend, and activist Vincent Harding, they both agreed that there was something more than mere coincidence at work.

It would not be the last time that Thurman and Martin Jr. crossed paths in significant ways. Was it accidental that Martin Luther King Jr., who read and wrote a paper about *Jesus and the Disinherited* during seminary, found the book so inspiring that he is said to have carried it with him every time he marched? Was it mere coincidence that Howard

Thurman accepted an appointment as a faculty member at Boston University—the same university where Dr. King was completing his doctoral work? Could it be described as happenstance that Martin Luther King attended many of Thurman's sermons at Marsh Chapel? Should we say it was simply chance that Coretta and Martin visited the Thurmans and that Howard and Martin spent time listening to the World Series in 1953 together and talking?

Divine assistance appears in the establishment of Fellowship Church as well. Traveling from Washington to San Francisco on a train in 1944, the Thurmans could book sleeper car accommodations only to Salt Lake City due to wartime limitations. During a casual conversation with a congenial fellow called Winthrop Martin, Thurman discovered he and his wife were returning from vacation and were heading to San Francisco also. The couple graciously shared the section they had booked, which allowed space for them all.

Upon further conversation, Thurman learned that Winthrop possessed expertise in public relations. Later Winthrop would volunteer as Fellowship Church's publicity chair, setting up all the promotion, including press coverage and a radio interview, for the congregation's opening celebration. This providential accident signaled to Thurman that the hand of God was operating to sustain him and his calling. With a deep trust in God, Thurman engaged in the tasks at hand—to yield to the Spirit of God who appeared to move him closer to his goals day by day. I believe that Howard Thurman prayed, listened, and opened his heart to God, thus attuning himself to frequencies of the Spirit in ways that many of us often miss.

LIFE-SAVING DISCERNMENT

For years I rarely thought to confer with anyone—let alone God—about my plans. I was goal driven, and I made major decisions about potential jobs and where to live based on my aims and the set of facts before me. Yet my faulty decision-making often yielded undesirable results, and I'd regret choices I'd made soon after making them. Over time, I began to seek counsel from the *inside* and to see the important role of discernment in decision-making. I began to rebalance the way I made choices, spending time in silence and prayer instead of just rushing forward into plans based on what appeared to yield the most success or status.

Once, having spent time in reflection in the quietness of the evergreens of the Great Smokey Mountains, I turned down an offer for an academic position at Swarthmore College. The answer I received during that time—a clear sense that I was not to take the job—made little sense to my family, friends, and colleagues. Some even questioned my mental health. Why would I turn down an excellent position without any guarantee that another would appear? Yet my Inner Guidance felt very forceful. I *knew* something about the move to Swarthmore didn't feel right even though I could not provide anyone with a logical reason.

Five years later, having accepted a job at the University of Colorado, Boulder, I sat in the examination room of a transplant surgeon, Dr. David Martin, in Denver. He explained to me what heart transplant surgery might entail. Casually he added, "Well, I guess you're lucky you're not living on the East Coast."

What? I inquired why. "On the East Coast, there are several transplant centers vying for the same organs. Out here there is less competition because the next transplant center is UCLA. The heart cannot live outside of the body for more than four hours. Given the high donor rate in Colorado and your blood type and body size, your wait shouldn't be long. If you were living in the Northeast, you might not receive an organ in time."

I sat there, speechless. I had turned down a job at Swarthmore, in Pennsylvania, not knowing at the time that I would ever need a heart transplant. Was this a remarkable coincidence or the result of the spiritual discernment I pursued in the mountains? I suspect that if I shared this story with Howard Thurman, he might add that the Spirit of God dances with each of us daily. It is our role to follow, like a partner.

DIVINE INTERVENTION GONE AWRY

The notion of divine intervention can become theologically confused and misused. Headlines shock us with portrayals of parents who withhold medication or hospitalization from their children or loved ones and of patients who terminate medical treatment because they believe God will intervene and heal them. For them, the disease is a test of faith by God, and children and adults often die as a result.

We often wonder why God doesn't intervene in our lives. Why didn't God save our mother or spouse when we had spent days praying? How could a beloved father or brother be struck down by a drunk driver while walking down the street? Are these cases of *unholy* coincidence? Another chilling example of misappropriating divine intervention is when a person blows up a building, church, synagogue, or temple, killing people and claiming they heard a voice from God directing them to do so.

So we must be careful about how we interpret coincidences, and we must be vigilant about what we call providence. Yet just because the concept of divine intervention can be misused doesn't mean we should stop seeing and naming God's work in the world. In the meditation "A Divinity that Shapes Our Ends," which begins this chapter, Thurman intimates that providential occurrences nudge us toward discovering and living out God's purpose for our lives. Pay attention, Thurman suggests: the involvement of God as Spirit is as common and as natural as the sun, birds, and trees outside. Could the Spirit of God be leading us toward wholeness? Our task may be to seek out and play our part in the plan for the restoration of the beloved creation. As we walk through decisions large and small, the voice of Howard Thurman advises us to notice and work with Spirit, who longs to guide us toward purposeful living.

REFLECTION QUESTIONS

- Have you had any experiences that you'd consider to be divine intervention, holy coincidence, sacred synchronicity, or providential accident? Which term do you connect with most?

- As you reflect on your life, do you notice any patterns of coincidence or serendipity that you hadn't thought of before?

- How have you utilized discernment or asked for help with decisions? How have you cultivated the patience to wait for confirmation?

- What holy coincidences in the life of someone else have led you to examine some of your own?

SPIRITUAL STEPS

- Make a list of coincidences or synchronicities and how they changed you and the direction of your life.

- For one day or one week or even longer—maybe forty days—listen to and follow your Inner Guidance. Instead of setting a schedule or making a to-do list, spend time each day quieting yourself and listening for Spirit's guidance.

- Keep a journal, similar to a dream journal, about sacred synchronicities. Where is Spirit trying to lead you?

- Find a quiet place outside—a park bench or a bench along a walking path. Ask Spirit a question that you would like answered. Observe when and how the answer appears.

CHAPTER 6

THE VERY HEART OF GOD

DISCOVER THE GENIUS IN THE RELIGION OF JESUS

Fundamental to all was his [Jesus's] deep confidence in God. This is the heart of what he gives to the disinherited. Here is no superficial optimism, but a vast faith that reaches through all dimensions of human life, giving dignity, worth, and purpose even to the least significant. In Jesus, all men may see the illumined finger of God guiding them in the way that they should go, so that high above the clash of arms in the conflict for status, for place, for privilege, for rights, he can hear speaking distinctly and clearly to his own spirit the still small voice of God.

—Howard Thurman, *The Mood of Christmas*

As a child, I didn't know how to feel about Jesus. In Catholic school, the nuns often lectured us about sinning—such as telling lies or disobeying our teachers and parents—and reminded us that Jesus died on the cross for our sins. So whenever I'd eat forbidden candy or disobey my parents, the guilt—Jesus had hung from the cross for *this?*—would seem unbearable.

I also learned that Jesus was God incarnate and therefore perfect and that I must be like him. As a seven-year-old, I wondered: how could I live up to such a high standard? Why would God send his son to earth to suffer and die? Did God dislike children? And what about little girls— what role did we play in the kingdom of God? Simple faith failed to satisfy my inquisitive mind, so Jesus remained an enigma.

I also couldn't reconcile the Jesus I heard about in the New Testament with the doctrines, creeds, rules, and regulations that many Christian denominations promoted. As a Catholic, I didn't read the Bible much, although a Gospel reading was central to every mass. I heard about a child born in a manger who became a brilliant teacher, told great stories, and was crucified on a cross for our sins. He preached outdoors on grassy hills or near lakes and rivers. He expressed love and kindness to all people, even the outcasts of his society. He healed masses of people. At the same time, the religion he founded branded me with original sin and called me unworthy from the start. The list of sins requiring penance seemed endless.

So keeping a cordial but distant relationship with Jesus, I entered young adulthood. For several years I attended church and especially loved gospel music, but I still felt indifferent toward Jesus. To me, he was the central figure in a liturgical calendar I followed mostly out of habit. Would I ever obtain the same fervor for Jesus that I observed in others at church?

Discovering Howard Thurman's classic book *Jesus and the Disinherited* was a game changer. It lifted the fog of my confusion by distinguishing between the religion *about* Jesus from the religion *of* Jesus. I remember that day clearly. My friend Joshua said that if I were to read anything by Thurman, I must read this book. So I ordered it and put it on a small bookshelf next to a green chaise lounge in our living room for a few weeks. I wanted to wait until I had a window of time to read and absorb it.

One sunny winter morning, as the sun peeked up over the eastern horizon, I picked it up. As I turned each page, sunlight streaming over my shoulder, I kept thinking, "Yes!" and "Now I understand why I was so perplexed about Jesus as a child." I felt like I was reading a novel with surprising plot twists. This short book, packed with startling insights, gave me a new take on Christianity, Jesus, and the struggles of Black folks and castes like them all over the world. *Jesus and the Disinherited* gave me a deeper understanding of Jesus's liberating and transformative spirituality.

For Thurman, Jesus of Nazareth became master, mentor, and guide, both human and divine, and "the grand prototype" for a real Christian. Howard Thurman had grappled with Christianity for much of his life. As a child, he pondered how this religion of Jesus might sustain him, like it had his grandmother and mother. As we saw earlier, his intellectually inclined father, Saul Thurman, did not belong to a church. When Saul died, the church branded Saul a sinner who died "outside of Christ." Ultimately, a visiting clergyman agreed to preach the funeral—yet took the opportunity to condemn Saul to hell. Howard, then seven years of age, knew the goodness of his father, and he felt bewildered by these events. Wandering the woods alone, he continued to muse over this religion that castigated the unchurched. Weren't love and character more important than mere churchgoing? What type of religion required racial separation during worship and allowed for the constant denigration of Black folks? Howard loved his solitary conversations with Jesus, and what he knew of him did not match with Christianity as he was seeing it practiced.

Howard Thurman read the Bible regularly to his grandmother, who could not read. His fascination with Grandma Nancy grew when she prohibited him from reading certain Pauline Letters, especially those passages commanding slaves to obey their masters. He carried these moments with him, and on occasion, he would wrestle with them under the oak tree in his backyard or in a sermon or lecture. Eventually Thurman would gather his insights into a little book, one that would serve as a spiritual blueprint for nonviolent protest and inspire millions of people—and actually change the course of American history.

CHRISTIANITY UNDER REVIEW

As Howard Thurman grew into adolescence, his intrigue with Jesus and Christianity swelled. He knew he needed to scrutinize the Gospels for himself. He often wrote and sometimes preached throughout college and seminary about the character of a true Christian and what aspects of the religion might appeal to Negroes. As early as 1928, Howard Thurman presented a series of lectures on Negro spirituals, which held hidden gems about the need to protect one's personality or self-concept. He encouraged students at Spelman and Morehouse to not let the repressive atmosphere destroy them. It was during this time that he began to see how Jesus engaged in nonviolent noncooperation with the Jewish and Roman hierarchies. The Gospels, it seemed, provided the ingredients to create a nonviolent religion.

The summer before his pilgrimage to India in 1935, Thurman published an article titled "Good News for the Underprivileged." In it he laid the groundwork for a perusal of traditional Christianity and how its theology contrasted with the message Jesus conveyed. Another source of his inquiry was the apostle Paul, whose understanding of Jesus's teachings seemed to deviate from what Jesus himself intended. Although a Jew, Paul possessed privileges as a Roman citizen. Thurman writes, "Why Paul could feel this way is quite clear, when we remember that he was a Jew—yes, but a free Jew. But Jesus was not a free Jew. If a Roman soldier kicked Jesus into a Galilean ravine, it was merely a Jew in the ravine. He could not appeal to Caesar."

In several books, Howard Thurman reports the conversation he shared with a Ceylonese lawyer on an early stop during his overseas travels. After Thurman's lecture at a law school, the lawyer invited him to his office for some tea. Sitting across from Thurman, the lawyer interrogated him about his links to Christianity—a religion, the lawyer argued, that supported slavery, noting that one of the slave ships was named *Jesus*. This religion of Thurman's, the lawyer said, justified lynching, segregation, colonialism, and imperialism. How could he possibly adhere to such a faith?

Somewhere the true meaning of Jesus's message had been corrupted to allow for the domination and separation of God's creation. Thurman adamantly insisted that he was a follower of the religion *of* Jesus. The true origin of Christianity, as practiced by Jesus, was genius because it spoke to the inherent holiness and worthiness of all that God created. Jesus taught that God's creation consists of everyone, including a wide array of marginalized individuals (such as people of color, women, and people with disabilities) as well as people of other faith traditions (Hindu, Muslim, Buddhist). When Thurman returned from India, he presented a series of lectures called "The Significance of Jesus." Some concepts in these lectures would later appear in *Jesus and the Disinherited.*

Together with Thurman, we ask now: Who was Jesus? And what did he say and do to inspire a religion adopted by billions?

THE SIGNIFICANCE OF JESUS

Howard Thurman was particularly intrigued with the person of Jesus—what some biblical scholars labeled "the historical Jesus," although he did not use this term. Thurman wanted to know: who was this person who appeared human yet so aware of his divinity?

In some lectures, Howard Thurman tackles the story of Jesus's temptation in the wilderness, a nature quest illustrating Jesus's rejection of materialism, power, and celebrity. Jesus knew that God was the Creator and Source of everything and the only entity deserving of worship. He promoted love, championing it as the greatest commandment. In fact, loving God and loving others took precedence over obeying an array of religious rules and regulations. Thurman then juxtaposes love with hate:

> *If we accept the general proposition that all life is one arising out of a communal center: God, all expression of love are acts of God. Hate, then, becomes a form of annihilation of self and others—in short, suicide. Violence is animal and atheistic because it denies the unity of life and defeats its maintenance and furthermore on the highest levels. It is for this reason that hatred and bitterness, self-violating as they seem to be, in the last analysis are apt to destroy both the hated and the hater. In Jesus' insistence that the normal ethical relationship between men is love, he reflects most accurately the very heart of God.*

Howard Thurman also highlighted Jesus's deep prayer life. Jesus prayed constantly until he uttered his last words on the cross. In his analysis of the Gospels, Thurman observed Jesus outside in nature engaging in daily solitary prayer, either in early mornings or late evenings. Particularly after healing and preaching to multitudes of people, Jesus escaped to the mountains for quiet. Thurman notes, "It seems in this prayer, as in so many of the others, Jesus needed to have his spirit restored and reinforced by basking himself in the complete presence of God." Jesus even instructed others to go to a quiet place and commune with God. Daily prayer as silent communion with God was common for Jesus because "to him God is the answer to the deepest needs of human life; and if I were as sure of God as Jesus was, God would become for me the answer to my deepest needs."

In two final lectures, Howard Thurman focused on the prophetic nature of the religion of Jesus and its reverence for life. Living out the "good news" that all that God created is worthy, Jesus was crucified not because he committed a crime but because with his teachings, sermons, and parables, Jesus challenged a social, political, and economic order that stigmatized and exploited dispossessed people like himself. Further, Thurman underscores how Jesus's instruction emphasizes a veneration for all that God created. Thurman concludes that discrimination of any kind is not the will of God. For Jesus, the will of God was primary. For every moment, every matter, the question for Jesus was "What is the will of God concerning this?" as opposed to "What will people say about me?" or "What is most expedient?"

With these essays, Howard Thurman leaves us with a penetrating query: What characterizes contemporary Christianity? Has it neglected the essential message of Jesus—about love, intimacy with God through silent, solitary prayer, worship of God alone, advocacy for the dignity and worth of all people, and reverence for God's holy creation?

JESUS AND THE DISINHERITED

Thurman was convinced that the church's disregard for the prophetic message of Jesus remained most costly for disenfranchised people. It is not surprising that early Christians failed to promote the social justice aspects of Jesus's teachings given the atmosphere of slaughter and annihilation. Later, the institutionalization of Christianity by the Roman Empire meant social justice would not play a prominent role. Yet Thurman found in the religion of Jesus answers to his long-pursued questions about how Negroes and other dispossessed people could live with dignity and humanity even under repressive and cruel conditions. He articulated this sentiment in the form of a question: "What do you do with the call in your heart from God if you are living in a situation of oppression?"

In 1949, Howard Thurman published *Jesus and the Disinherited*, which outlined these powerful insights. Thurman wanted the term "disinherited" to be part of the book's title, since his intent was to inspire colonized and oppressed people on and beyond American soil, including those embroiled in the anticolonial struggles in Africa, India, and Asia during the 1940s. *Disinherited* is an apt description for people whom dominant Christianity had literally cast out. The disinherited belonged to a caste, as Isabel Wilkerson brilliantly delineates in *Caste: The*

Origins of our Discontents—one that dominant Christianity had deemed unequal and unacceptable. In *Jesus and the Disinherited,* Thurman returns to that lawyer's question: how could enslaved or colonized people embrace the same religion practiced by the people who subjugated and denigrated them?

Writing during the Jim Crow era, Thurman poses a set of questions in the preface. What relevance would the disinherited—"people who stand with their backs against the wall"—find in the religion of Jesus? How does the religion *of* Jesus differ from Christianity, the religion *about* Jesus? Thurman notes that his considerations are both personal and professional. He yearned to offer hope and resolve to his deeply wounded people, who experienced daily systemic and personal degradation.

Howard Thurman found dominant Christianity unable to cope with issues of discrimination with respect to race, religion, and national origin. He wondered whether this inability was a weakness at the heart of the religion or rather a breach of Jesus's original teachings. Christianity also appeared to place emphasis on the future—on heaven, where the disinherited would be released from their suffering. White Christian leaders, using the Bible, implored Negroes during the slavery and post-slavery eras to just be patient. Wait until the next life for freedom, human rights, and personal respect, they said. But Thurman knew Jesus taught that the kingdom of God is at hand. The kingdom of God is present now.

What is most brilliant about Thurman's analysis is his amplification of the stark parallels between Jesus's context, as a poor, marginalized Jew living in Palestine, and the social, political, and economic milieu of American Negroes. In order to survive, most disinherited people—enslaved people and their descendants, sharecroppers, domestics, farmworkers, refugees, immigrants, and the undocumented—feel compelled to offer unmerited flattery to those in authority. But Jesus knew that powerful people—oppressors, specifically—were not the gods that disinherited people needed to worship or depend on.

Luther Smith Jr. adeptly summarizes how Thurman interprets the religion of Jesus: Jesus stood with the dispossessed because he was one of them. Jesus's message provided a vital resource to empower his own people, who felt disenfranchised, vulnerable, disrespected, and without a stable sense of self.

JESUS AS SPIRITUAL PSYCHOLOGIST

In the first chapter of *Jesus and the Disinherited*, Howard Thurman highlights the lack of association between the form of Christianity and the person of Jesus. Many people forget that Jesus was not Christian but Jewish, and Thurman reminds us that it was not his intention to start a religion. Notably, Jesus did not preach to the Jewish aristocracy. He shared company with social pariahs such as tax collectors and prostitutes. Jesus spoke to stigmatized Samaritans and healed the son of a Roman soldier, a member of the dominant group. Jesus promoted the inherent worthiness of all people. As a traveling country preacher, he held gatherings mostly outside and interpreted the Jewish faith in new and relevant ways.

Howard Thurman understood Jesus, without directly labeling him as such, to be a spiritual and psychological genius. Jesus knew real power lay in the inward center—the inner life of an individual—and it was here that Jesus directed his attention. Comprehending both the spiritual and psychological dynamics of the self, Jesus offered a solution far more powerful than a mere political uprising. "He recognized with authentic realism that anyone who permits another to determine the quality of his inner life gives into the hands of the other the keys to his destiny," Thurman writes. "If a man knows precisely what he can do to you or what epithet he can hurl against you in order to make you lose your temper, your equilibrium, then he can always keep you under subjection. It is a man's reaction to things that determines their ability to exercise power over him."

The first time I read *Jesus and the Disinherited*, I paused when I got to this section. I put the book down and went for a walk outside. Questions began to bubble up in my mind. How often had I allowed someone's unfounded attacks or spiteful actions to sap my confidence and immobilize me? Was I in charge of my inner life, or did I permit others to control my inner world? Could the inner life—the inner sanctuary that Howard Thurman speaks about elsewhere—be key to psychological and spiritual freedom?

PAUL THE ROMAN CITIZEN

Howard Thurman argues that the status of the apostle Paul as a Roman citizen and the privileges that accrued to him as a result matter. Predictably, Paul viewed the world through a very different lens than Jesus did, particularly when it came to power, social status, and politics. Paul admonished people to obey a repressive government he felt was ordained by God, and he believed one must earn their way into the kingdom of God.

Vincent Harding, renowned historian, civil rights activist, developer of Black theological thought, and close companion of Howard Thurman in later years, also questioned Paul's role in refashioning Jesus's message. In the foreword to the 1996 edition of *Jesus and the Disinherited*, Harding wonders if the apostle Paul and others who wrote about Jesus many years after his death and resurrection modified the true meaning of Jesus.

For Thurman, the shift Paul introduced led to a tragedy for Christianity, for it evolved into a religion adopted and sanctioned by the government. Christianity sustained imperialism and colonialism both in the United States and throughout the world. It supported slave traders, slaveholders, Jim Crow enforcers, and organizations like the Ku Klux Klan.

African Americans and other disinherited people, Thurman writes, need to know that the true message of Jesus centers on love, intrinsic worthiness, prayer, and the worship of the living God. God, as the Creator and Source of all, would desire justice and humanity for every segment of creation.

THREE HOUNDS THAT TRACK THE DISINHERITED

A powerful group cannot overtake and dominate people without winning control over their minds and their spirits. Howard Thurman believed Jesus wanted to raise the awareness of other poor Jews by modeling for them a direct connection to God. In Jesus's time, to make a sacrifice to God at the temple required money—for an animal to sacrifice, temple fees, and Roman taxes—that poor Jews didn't have or that would take them many days of labor to earn. Everywhere people tried to find ways to earn favor with anyone in the temple hierarchy, and exploitation was rampant.

Thurman writes that Jesus taught people that the three hounds that track the trail of the disinherited—fear, hypocrisy, and hatred—need not leave them powerless. They must not allow these responses to power to prevent them from employing God's power to survive in such circumstances.

FEAR

People who are oppressed live in a constant state of fear. Howard Thurman outlines several types of fears that plague them. Lack of income causes people to fear being hungry and homeless. Fear of violence prevails because violence is frequently sanctioned by the government. This fact saddened Thurman. Harming or killing a person based on their caste ignores their personhood and symbolizes the ultimate act of dehumanization. In contemporary society, random violence that targets people of color exacerbates the pervasive fear of all disinherited people. An unarmed Black motorist stopped and killed by police, a workplace raided to search for those who are undocumented, an Asian person attacked while walking down the street, a young Black man out for an afternoon jog tracked down and murdered by white men: each instance increases the fear.

What Thurman extracted from Jesus's teaching was similar to what he learned from his mother and grandmother: claiming one's birthright as a holy child of God creates a sense of dignity and determination. "The prophetic nature of the religion of Jesus says God cares for everything including little old me!" Thurman writes. And like Jesus, Thurman typically turned inward to the stillness of God to assuage his apprehensions. Leaders in the civil rights movement, despite their fears of violence and arrest, strategized with the certainty of God undergirding their convictions. They taught participants how vital it was to turn inward before marching and protesting, to acknowledge the fear but allow their faith to move them forward, to take each step. The practice of radical trust in God, of going inward—of centering down—before confronting outward violence became an essential component of nonviolent protest training.

HYPOCRISY

Defenseless people often protect themselves against the strong by finding creative ways to fool them. Howard Thurman describes the use of deception by the disinherited, acknowledging that anyone who lacks power typically utilizes it. But to offer someone unmerited flattery based on their power status serves no one. Thurman cites South African activist Olive Schreiner, who wrote about the need for women to engage in constant manipulation in male-dominated societies.

What is the consequence when falsity masquerades as truth? Howard Thurman writes, "If a man continues to call a good thing bad, he will eventually lose his sense of moral distinctions. . . . That is to say, the fact that the lives of the disinherited are lightly held by the dominant group tends to create the same attitude the dispossessed hold toward each other." The thinking goes, if the government lacks a moral compass and dehumanizes people, why should I respect life? Elsewhere Thurman points to the constant thwarting disinherited people suffer because they cannot realize their potential or be their authentic selves. They displace their utter frustration on each other. This internal disorganization of self may account for acts of random violence in marginalized communities.

This insight—that the use of violence against racially and ethnically profiled people tends to disorganize them from within—first emerged in Thurman's article "Good News for the Underprivileged." Gandhi's articulation of the same idea in their meeting only affirmed Thurman's convictions.

In Thurman's interpretation of Jesus's teachings, earnestness and authenticity must characterize our lives. He describes it this way: "Unwavering sincerity says that man should always recognize the fact that he lives always in the presence of God, always under the divine scrutiny. . . . From him [God] nothing is hidden." Jesus demanded sincerity, and he was particularly critical of hypocrisy.

HATRED

Hatred in the disinherited for those who dominate and exploit them is born out of bitterness or sustained resentment. It's not uncommon for white people to ask, "Why are Black people so angry?" Some think African Americans should simply be grateful slavery is over. Others express astonishment that African Americans do not harbor greater hate and bitterness.

Howard Thurman would say an initial expression of hatred is actually a useful sign—an indication that a disinherited person is awakening. To accept and internalize one's devaluation is to remain blind to one's holiness and unity with all that God created. As their consciousness grows, hatred is a stage the dispossessed pass through on the way to claiming their birthright as holy children of God. Anger and animosity fuel the walk toward inner and outer freedom. Yet sustained acrimony and rancor can become debilitating. Even insufferable people are holy children of God, though they may not recognize it. Thurman writes, "To love such people requires an uprooting of the bitterness of betrayal, the heartiest poison that grows in the human spirit."

How do we reconcile with our enemies—people who hate us and treat us with contempt and violence? Thurman details what Jesus says about relationships with possible adversaries, beginning with the personal enemy. You have a dispute or miscommunication with a relative or friend—someone who resides in your inner circle. Jesus instructs us to reunite with our sisters and brothers before offering our gifts to God.

Another type of enemy makes it difficult for certain groups to live without shame and humiliation. In Jesus's time, these were the tax collectors—the ultimate victimizers. They collected exorbitant taxes on behalf of the empire. Who could love them? Yet Jesus saw each tax collector as a holy child of God.

The third type of enemy is people who represent the institutions that systematically betray the will of God through economic exploitation, psychological denigration, and social exclusion. For Jesus, these were the Romans. But Jesus taught that even a Roman needed to be perceived as a person. "Love and pray for your enemy, that you may be children of your father who is in heaven" (Matthew 5:44–45). This same principle lies at the heart of nonviolent direct action.

Howard Thurman noticed that Jesus modeled the path of love. We often see this evocation of love during natural disasters, when strangers rush to rescue everyone. Love overcomes hate. We see this same premise in one of Dr. Martin Luther King Jr.'s famous books, *The Strength to Love*. Vincent Harding notes that *Jesus and the Disinherited* was published after Thurman had cofounded the first intentionally interracial congregation, the Church of the Fellowship of All Peoples in San Francisco. Thurman witnessed the worship of God by people of a variety of racial and ethnic backgrounds and the freedom and power that accompanies fellowship without human-imposed barriers.

Under no conditions should anyone, especially dispossessed people, remain psychologically and spiritually imprisoned by fear, hypocrisy, and hatred. Thurman concludes his book with this counsel: real love can occur only among "freed spirits."

INTERPERSONAL POWER RELATIONSHIPS

When I finished reading *Jesus and the Disinherited*, I realized that Jesus's life and teachings as interpreted by Howard Thurman offered an eternal spirituality—a roadmap to a place of psychological and spiritual freedom for everyone. Although he intended the book for the disinherited, the same attributes that track them also characterize the weaker person in any power relationship, not only those locked in caste systems. Employees are often afraid of their supervisors, for example, and may act in obsequious ways or develop bitterness and hate toward them. In many relationships—husband–wife, parent–child, teacher–student—the less powerful person often fears or even hates the more powerful person and yet attempts to cajole them to obtain something: the end of abuse, the freedom to pursue a particular career, a favorable grade, a raise, or a living wage. Could the same principles Howard Thurman underscores about the religion of Jesus liberate any people who find themselves powerless?

Biblical scholar and professor Mitzi J. Smith describes the survival skills needed to transform and transcend power relationships. Dipping into the well of power and courage within us, we strengthen our resolve to not allow anyone or anything to disturb our composure. "Strong enough means one is not overcome with or driven by fear, does not resort to hatred, is never deceptive and loves one's enemies," Smith argues. As Howard Thurman illustrates, Jesus speaks to the importance of being aware of and working on the inward center.

Equipped with a fortified inner spirit and deep belief that God cares, we can absorb the vicissitudes of life. This inner freedom requires a radical trust and deep intimacy with God. Thurman affirms this position with this statement: "Instead of relation between the weak and the strong there is merely a relationship between human beings. A man is a man, no more, no less. The awareness of this fact marks the supreme moment of human dignity."

FREE AT LAST

The liberating spirituality of Jesus, as outlined by Thurman, is life-changing. Having read *Jesus and the Disinherited* several times now, I believe the Gospels proclaim good news for everyone but *especially* for the disinherited and forgotten. They offer freedom and empowerment simultaneously.

Yet the good news also makes demands to love everyone, including those who oppress and brutalize. "When we love, that is what we do," Thurman writes. "It says, meet people where they are and treat them as if they were where they ought to be, and by so doing, we believe them into the fulfillment of their possibilities and love becomes an act of redemption. . . . Love of this sort places a crown over the head of another who is always trying to grow tall enough to wear it."

On March 23, 1940, after being arrested for refusing to sit on a broken seat on a Greyhound bus in St. Petersburg, Virginia, Pauli Murray, along with her friend Adelene Brown, were thrown into a dank, foul-smelling jail cell with grimy mattresses filled with bedbugs. Allowed to keep a single notebook, Murray spilled her ideas about creative nonviolence onto the page. When she and Adelene acted with equanimity, remained courteous, and pressed for humane treatment, they practiced the spirit of Gandhi's method of *satyagraha*, or "truth force." Their peaceful conduct moved their jailers and the other prisoners. Historian Anthony Siracusa shares this insight about Pauli Murray: "She recalled that Gandhi had been imprisoned seven times since the start of the Second World War and noted that the Indian civil disobedience campaigns had at their heart 'a willingness to sacrifice for your ideal—to change [the] heart of [the] enemy.' Murray wrote that India seemed to have a 'well-disciplined movement' that grew from the ancient religious traditions where a concern for the enemy was deeply rooted and sincere."

Jesus and the Disinherited inspired a host of readers in the immediate aftermath of its publication and in the decades to come. Bayard Rustin, James Farmer, James Lawson, Martin Luther King Jr., John Lewis, Jesse Jackson, Vernon Jordan, Whitney Young, Andrew Young, Marian Wright Edelman, Vincent Harding: these and other prominent leaders in the civil rights movement in America found living wisdom in its pages. The book spoke to many oppressed people throughout the world, and it continues to reach through history to awaken and stir us to action now.

REFLECTION QUESTIONS

- In what situations do you find yourself susceptible to the three hounds—fear, deception, and hatred?

- Who do you find most challenging to love?

- What differences do you see between the "religion *about* Jesus" and the "religion *of* Jesus"?

- In what ways do you need to strengthen your inward center?

SPIRITUAL STEPS

- Think about the spirituality of Jesus—the promotion of love and reconciliation, intimacy with God with quiet listening, advocacy for the dignity and worth of all people, and reverence for all of God's creation. Take one or more of these practices and make it a spiritual discipline.

- Who is on your list of enemies? Pray about what you might say and then take action toward reconciliation by calling, writing, or meeting them.

- Take a walk and consider what Howard Thurman says about the condition of the disinherited and oppressed people in the United States and all over the world.

CHAPTER 7

THE MEANING OF ALL THINGS

EMBRACE MYSTICISM FOR COMPASSIONATE SOCIAL ACTION

*There is the rest of detachment and withdrawal when the spirit
moves into the depths of the region of the Great Silence. . . . Here
the Presence of God is sensed as an all pervasive aliveness which
materializes into the concreteness of communion: the reality of
prayer. Here God speaks without words and the self listens without ears. Here at last, glimpses of the meaning of all things and
the meaning of one's own life are seen with all their strivings.*
—Howard Thurman, *The Inward Journey*

I sit in a cushioned gold and red accent chair in my living
room, while David sits on the couch. We meet here each
month for spiritual companioning, and today David says
he needs to share a recent mystical encounter. I read one of

Howard Thurman's meditations out loud, and then we take a moment of silence.

David opens his eyes. I sip my tea and listen to David's story. "It's early in the morning, around 6:30 a.m.," he says. "I turned on the light that sits next to my CPAP machine on the nightstand. It was still dark, and while sitting in bed, I read Psalm 118:8—'It is better to take refuge in the Lord than to put confidence in mortals,'" David says. "Then I started singing a song: 'I'm going to trust in the Lord, I'm going to trust in the Lord, I'm going to trust in the Lord until I die.'"

He pauses, looking for the words to describe what happened next. "All of a sudden, it's like the song started singing itself in my mind. I lacked the power to stop it."

I smile and signal him to continue. "A deep, heavy, slow presence came over me," he says. "I labored to slow down my breathing. There was a heavy weight on my chest. God spoke as slow as molasses. It was like sticky, gooey love running down the wall of my being, coating me, warming me, with love. I couldn't control it, and at the same time I didn't want it to end. He told me not to worry about my life. God told me it was about love. It begins with love and it ends with love, and in the middle we must be love. It is our only hope. God said to do what you can and trust me."

We sit in silence for a moment. "I'm still trying to make sense of it," David says, shaking his head. "I thought you might be able to help me understand it."

I hear stories like David's more often than I did fifteen years ago, when I began my practice of spiritual direction. I notice a yearning from more and more people for intimacy with God. I don't know how to explain why I hear more of these stories of encounters with a Presence than I used to. But I accept each story, each account of a mystical experience, as a gift.

It is difficult, if not impossible, to *make* a religious experience of God like David's happen. We can't force encounters. Howard Thurman believed, however, that certain conditions would increase their likelihood. Practices such as listening prayer or meditation, quiet and solitude, and even suffering can lead us to an awareness of the presence of God or Spirit.

EVERYDAY MYSTICS

As a seminary student walking home late one night, Thurman noticed the sound of water. He had taken this route many times, and he had never heard even a drip. The next day Thurman discussed his observations with one of his professors, who told him that a canal ran underneath the street. Because the noises of streetcars, automobiles, and passersby were absent late at night, Howard could discern the sound of water.

Thurman equates these sounds, which had prevented him from hearing the water, to the inner chatter within our minds that prevents us from being aware of God's presence. Quieting the surface noise in our minds is what Thurman urges us to do when he instructs us, as he does throughout his writings, to "center down."

What attracts and holds our attention determines how and when we will experience God. "In the total religious experience we learn how to wait; we learn how to ready the mind and the spirit," he writes. "It is in the waiting, brooding, lingering, tarrying timeless moments that the essence of the religious experience becomes fruitful. It is here that I learn to listen and to swing wide the very doors of my being, to clean out the corners and crevices of my life so that when His presence invades, I am free to enjoy His coming to Himself in me." Thurman believed this activity may also require letting go of hatred and bitterness so that in coming into your center, you are coming into God as the Creator of existence because "God bottoms existence."

Thurman demystified mysticism by framing it simply. Mystics are people who have a personal religious experience or an encounter with God. This description has freed me and many others from thinking that God appears to people only after years of prayer and living an ascetic, isolated life. Thurman believed anyone can be a mystic if they are open to the experience. He opened a door to a world where mystics move freely among us and live ordinary lives. Mystics are the ones who can hear the water flowing beneath the street. They know how to quiet the surface noise enough to hear the meaning of all things coursing below daily life.

Everyday mystics are people who commune with the presence of God, receive guidance through prophetic visions, voices, and dreams, and commit themselves to living for God rather than solely for themselves. Their vision for life is larger and more expansive, knowing that they are alive for a reason, a purpose that will benefit human spirits they may never meet. Although he did not publicly declare himself a mystic, Thurman lived out an identity grounded in mysticism, as he regularly felt oneness with God and on occasion experienced visions. He also believed that mystical moments should stir people toward love, community, and social action.

FROM MYSTIC TO SCHOLAR OF MYSTICISM

Howard Thurman shared widely about his mystical encounters as a young boy, as we saw in chapters 1 and 2. But it wasn't until he picked up the book *Following the Trail of Life* by Rufus Jones that he felt compelled to embark upon a formal investigation of mysticism. Spending a semester with Jones, immersed in the study of Plato, Augustine, Meister Eckhart, St. Francis of Assisi, and French Quietest Madame Guyon, Thurman found his thinking about mysticism, religion, and spirituality transformed.

Like Thurman, Rufus Jones grew up aware of the presence of God outdoors. His mystical life began with daily family morning worship. He writes,

> *Every day after breakfast, we had a long period of family silent worship, during which all the older members of the group seemed to be plainly communing in joyous fellowship with a real Presence. The reality of it all was so great, and the certainty of something more than just ourselves in the room was so clearly felt that we little folks were caught into the experience and carried along with the others. The mystical hush had its own awe and the rapt look on*

the older faces deepened the sense of awe and won-
der. By the time I was four years old, I had formed the
habit of using corporate silence in a heightening and
effective way. It brought with it, even for the child, a
sense of Presence.

Thus both Rufus Jones and Howard Thurman were initi-
ated into mysticism long before they began their systematic
examination of it. They used their personal experiences to
inform their thinking and writing, which made mysticism
more accessible to spiritual seekers like me. They provided
everyday people with the vocabulary and tools to describe
mystical encounters.

KINDS OF MYSTICISM

Many people are familiar with negation mysticism even if
they don't know the term. Negation mystics seek isolation
and often withdraw from social life. They yearn for union
with God, and others think of them as exceptional or holy
people. Through constant prayer and work, often within
a cloistered religious community, negation mystics devote
themselves to God in private ways.

Rufus Jones introduced Howard Thurman to affirmation
mysticism. Jones felt strongly that there was a "distinction
between cloistered, world-denying mysticism and a positive
mysticism that embraced the world and its concerns." He
perceived the latter form of mysticism to be characteristic
of George Fox and most Quakers. When these mystics go
inside themselves to God, they come up into community, or

oneness. Affirmative mystics yearn to perpetuate the feeling of wholeness that encompasses them in fleeting moments of communion with God. These unitive moments trigger a response: a gnawing need to eliminate barriers like immoral, unethical, and unjust conditions.

Many people believed that Rufus Jones created a personal mysticism—a mysticism for the masses. "He contended that the effects of genuine interior mystical experience are exteriorly reflected, that is to say, socially, ethically, and politically manifested in the relationship which obtains between the mystic and the world," writes Thurman scholar Alton Pollard. Pollard writes that Jones's notion of personal religion—his understanding of religion as experience and of the need to approach social questions from the vantage of personal religious experience or mysticism—was his great gift to Howard Thurman.

In one brief semester, Howard Thurman learned and absorbed an enormous amount of knowledge from Rufus Jones and considered him one of his greatest teachers. But he discovered Jones held little respect or tolerance for non-Christian mystics, including Hindu mystics like Gandhi. He also noticed that though Jones espoused and practiced affirmation mysticism, it centered on a form of pacifism that addressed anti-war efforts and international affairs. Jones did not apply affirmation mysticism to domestic issues like legalized segregation, discrimination, and violence against African Americans, nor did he address issues of low-wage textile workers. Many Quaker schools, including Haverford, where Jones taught, were some of the last to desegregate.

Thurman decided to accept Jones with all his contra-dictions and "ambivalences," as Thurman termed them. He writes that Jones helped him understand experiences he had lacked words to describe and introduced him to the concept of mysticism. "[Another] contribution that he made to me was to help me block out the territory that for the rest of my life I would be exploring," Thurman writes. "So, I tolerated my feelings and forgave me of my negative feelings because I didn't ever feel that he could ever get off the dime and deal, make the Quakers practice religion with the Negroes. I just—forgave him. . . . I will always love him because he opened a way in my thinking."

But Thurman knew he would need to carve out his own version of affirmation mysticism. He first shared his knowledge and understanding of mysticism in 1934, as part of a book review. He discussed the wide variety of people labeled as mystics, and he attributed much of the apprehen-sion about mysticism to the ways mystics understand and describe their experiences. Their attempts to articulate in simple language an indescribable event frequently resulted in cryptic and incomprehensible accounts. In later writ-ings, Thurman provides a working definition of mysticism as "the response of the individual to a personal encounter with God within his own spirit."

Thurman observed different kinds of mystics. One group consists of Catholic, Protestant, and some Hindu mystics, who see mystical experience as a part of their per-sonal relationship with God. God breaks through the veil to bring them a special message. Their encounters might lead to more prayer and intimacy with God. "Christ mystics," or those whose mystical experience centers on Jesus, compose a subset of this group. A second group of mystics holds a more intellectual sense of the Infinite. Some Greek philosophy and early Christian theology, the Way of the Tao, Neo-Platonism, Spinoza, and the Kabbalah belong in this group. These mystics and schools of mysticism desire to dissect the experience, to explore the enigmatic in a philosophical sense. How does mystical experience happen, and what does it reveal about God and the mysteries of life? A third cluster, the "Light Within" mystics, believe that divine rays of light reside within everyone and that we must obey with conviction the "still small Voice" of the Holy Spirit. Thurman would have included himself in this category, along with most Quakers and Meister Eckhart. Actions of Light Within mystics often link mysticism and social action, which we'll look at in more detail in the next chapter. A fourth category, then, includes mystics who associate themselves with the occult and deal with magic or attempt to acquire occult power through numerology or psychic endeavors.

Intimate contact with God gives mystics a sense of being at home with all existence. A mystic may gain a vision of God's purposes, and in response, begin to work to fulfill those goals.

MYSTICISM AND SOCIAL CHANGE

Howard Thurman sympathized with the bewilderment many Black people held about mysticism, as he was ridiculed for such thinking and writing. Many prominent Negro religious leaders associated mysticism with the occult and devil worship, while Negro social and political leaders felt it was impractical. How could mysticism alleviate the plight of segregation and oppression? They desired tools for liberation. In order to elevate the term "mysticism" and to educate people about its transformative powers, Thurman framed many lectures and sermons around the theme "Mysticism and Social Change." In 1939, in his first lecture series on mysticism, he presented talks to the Eden Theological Seminary on the following subjects: "Mysticism—An Interpretation," "Mysticism and Symbolism," "Mysticism and Ethics," and "Mysticism and Social Change."

About the affirmation mystic, Thurman writes, "He knows that he cannot escape in mere asceticism even as he recognizes its merits. He must embrace the social whole and seek to achieve empirically the good which has possessed him in his moment of profoundest insight. In his effort to do this, he constantly checks his action by insight. It keeps his insight true and his actions valid." This process involves surrender, for mystics are called to share with others the power that comes from union with God and to be merciful with others who continue to struggle along the spiritual path. Thurman would later discuss surrender as one of the disciplines of the spirit. The mystic yields, he writes, "the nerve center of his consent to a purpose or cause, a movement or an ideal, which may be more important to him than whether he lives or dies." Yielding one's heart to God results in feeding the need for wholeness, the longing to return to one's origins.

Scholar Alton Pollard argues that Thurman's "overall approach to mysticism and social change was significantly affected by the growing debate over the inability of Christianity to extricate itself from social conventions—conventions that openly victimized large segments of the population." Because Thurman's mysticism focused not only on the individual but also on the individual as part of a community, Pollard labels Thurman a "mystic-activist."

CREATIVE ENCOUNTER

Howard Thurman's exploration of mysticism as a religious experience continued throughout his life. He believed that encounters with God were natural and that "religious experience" and "creative encounter" better described the sensation of meeting God. In *The Creative Encounter*, Thurman draws a picture for us of how a person moves from a private encounter with God to a more transformative state. The evolution involves a shift in one's centeredness from the world to God. This change may entail certain spiritual disciplines such as prayer, commitment (or surrender, as we just saw), solitude, and suffering. The person emerges from the experience with a change in awareness. Thurman articulates it in this way:

> The central fact in religious experience is the awareness of meeting God. The descriptive words are varied: sometimes it is called an encounter; sometimes,

a confrontation; and sometimes, a sense of Presence. What is insisted upon, however, without regard to the term used, is that in the experience defined as religious, the individual is seen as being exposed to direct knowledge of ultimate meaning, ne plus ultra being, in which all that the individual is, becomes clear as immediate and often distinct revelation. He is face to face with something which is so much more, and so much more inclusive, than all of his awareness of himself that for him, in the moment, there are no questions. Without asking, somehow he knows.

The mind apprehends the whole—the experience is beyond or inclusive of the discursive. . . . The individual in the experience seems to come into possession of what he has known as being true all along. The thing that is new is the realization. *And this is of profound importance.*

In later writings, Thurman quotes from an essay written by Charles Bennett, who proposes that the mystic doesn't have a discovery of God but more a "rediscovery of the eternal" that was always present.

MYSTICISM AND NEUROTHEOLOGY

Remarkably, Howard Thurman spoke of neurotheology decades before it became a serious topic of scientific inquiry. He proposed that each time we have an encounter with God, structures in our brains actually change. "The central question here is, can the repetition of the religious experience bring about such a reconditioning of the patterns of behavior within the organism and neurological structure as to make the organism itself expressive of the insight derived from the repeated experience?" Thurman writes. "It would seem that as such a gradual structural change becomes operative, and is accompanied by a new or at least a different point of view; that is, a different conscious attitude toward life, toward experience, and toward people. It may be argued that the attitude comes first in a direct line from the religious experience and that such attitudes become the tutors of the nervous system and reconditioning process."

Some religious scholars and theologians might contend that he is speaking merely of conversion, but Thurman believed it was much more. An inner modification that results in an outer shift in perspective and even perception: this is why a person who has a mystical, religious, or creative encounter is never the same. If the encounters continue and repeat, a permanent change occurs.

TEXTURES OF MYSTICAL EXPERIENCES

Until I read Howard Thurman's meditations and autobiography, I had never considered myself a mystic. Yet as I reflect on my many still moments outside, during meditation, and lying in hospital beds in the early morning, I realize that I, too, have felt minutes of oneness, or a Presence nearby. Not all my mystical experiences are of an exceptional nature, but sometimes I sense that my body disappears in some way, and I feel a connection with everything and everyone.

My most extraordinary mystical encounters came about a month before my heart transplant. I awoke from a long, deep nap, and while still in a liminal state between sleep and waking, I became conscious of a Presence in the room. I didn't detect any visual image or form, but I felt It. I was a part of the Presence, and It was a part of me—there was no boundary. Without any words, I *knew* I could ask the Presence questions, and I could *feel* the answers. I peppered It with requests about when I needed to have the transplant. I learned through this unspoken communication that I could spend the Christmas holidays with my family but that after New Year's, I *must* go on the organ transplant list. Then the Presence vanished. I underwent a heart transplant on January 9, 1995. The transplant journey became the bedrock of a momentous spiritual awakening, one that only intense physical suffering engenders.

"Despite the personal character of suffering, the sufferer can work his way through to community," Thurman writes. "This does not make his pain less, but it does make it inclusive of many other people. Sometimes he discovers through the ministry of his own burden a larger comprehension of his fellows, of whose presence he becomes aware in his darkness. They are companions along the way."

COVERT MYSTICS

Naila sits across the video call screen seated at a desk in a makeshift office that also serves as her dining room. She wears large black headphones that match her black-rimmed glasses. As a seminary student in training to become a chaplain, Naila attended one of my Howard Thurman retreats and left wondering if she was a mystic. Later she contacted me about becoming her spiritual companion.

In one of our initial meetings, she explains her dilemma. "I have predictive dreams," she tells me tentatively. "Sometimes I know when someone is going to die. The intensity of the colors in the dreams indicate if death is imminent or in months. I don't know what to do with these dreams, and my former spiritual director, a priest, refused to discuss this part of my spiritual life."

I wait for her to say more. "Also, God talks with me," she continued. "We converse regularly, but there aren't many people I can talk to about these conversations and the love I feel for God and God feels for me." I ask Naila if she knows of any other people in her family who might also possess such gifts. "My grandmother," Naila replies. "She told me I had a gift and it was okay. But she is not a religious or spiritual authority, and I wonder, if I am a mystic, is that okay?"

Many people are afraid to disclose their mystical inclinations or spiritual gifts. In my experience as a spiritual director and companion, I listen to story after story about religious leaders—pastors, priests, rabbis, imams, and others—who dismiss mystical accounts or change the subject when people bring up such topics.

Confusion and apprehensiveness haunt covert mystics. Some fear their predictive dreams, visitations, or experiences of hearing the "voice of God," and they try to prevent or escape from these creative encounters. On occasion, covert mystics like Naila visit caring relatives or elders, such as grandmothers or aunts, who share their own spiritual tales.

Howard Thurman does not specifically address covert mystics, but I have a hunch that he would have advised them to find a trusted companion with whom to share such experiences. A creative encounter is a rare treasure, and one not to be wasted because of fear of ostracism. Working with Spirit, we can allow religious experiences to heal and awaken us. We can allow such encounters to, as Thurman would have said, spark a sense of the presence of God in others.

MYSTIC-ACTIVISTS

Thurman's life and writings on mysticism confirmed that we don't have to take monastic vows or accept a call to the ministry in order to bask in the loving presence of God. They also clarify how our encounters with God contribute to an inner resilience. Living as an ordinary mystic invites us to take our awareness of God with us into the emergency or operating room, the classroom, meetings, and courageous conversations. Spirit becomes a flowing stream of constant guidance that we can tap into by pausing and listening.

In his writings Thurman distinguishes between mysticism and social change, but he believed both were essential. In a tribute written by the esteemed Quaker mysticism scholar Douglas Steere, he commends Thurman to readers for his "concern for inward journeys that meet something at the center, which turns them outward again." Steere adds that Thurman must have carried in his heart this aphorism from Meister Eckhart: "You can only spend in good works what you have earned in contemplation." We need regular quiet time with God in order to have the strength, courage, and vitality required for social action: for moving against injustices, speaking truth to power, and assisting in humanitarian efforts.

Thurman believed Jesus was a mystic. "Mystical consciousness was part of Jesus' life," he writes. "It deepened his sense of self and his intimacy with God. Jesus' whole identity depended upon his mystical experiences. These experiences made him sure of God's presence, love, and commission for a ministry of love." Like Jesus, Howard Thurman lived his identity as a mystic-activist. He pressed for an active mysticism, for when we meet God, God has a role for each of us in the restoration of the beloved creation.

When people hear the word "activism," many think of marches and protests in the street. Yet not all participants in major human rights struggles like the civil rights movement marched. People cooked meals, babysat children, wrote and filed legal briefs, trained marchers, and became community organizers. Others who were unable to march prayed, made phone calls, and hosted movement gatherings. Activism can be anything that helps to heal people and the world. The call one hears in a unitive moment might involve work on gender or environmental justice concerns or humanitarian crises. It might mean working in a soup kitchen or connecting with military veterans or tutoring children. Or it might mean playwriting, choreography, painting, or sculpting.

Mystical experiences can give people a sense of vitality and lead them to their holy assignments. Part of Howard Thurman's response to God was to provide the spiritual and philosophical underpinnings for the work that calls people to action. Thurman "participated at the level that shapes the philosophy that creates the march," says Otis T. Moss II. "Without that, people don't know what to do before they march, while they march, or after they march."

Social action, writes Thurman, "is an expression of resistance against whatever tends to, or separates one from, the experience of God, who is the very ground of his being. . . . The mystic's concern with the imperative of social action is not merely to improve the conditions of society. It is not merely to feed the hungry, not merely to relieve human suffering and human misery. If this were all, in and of itself, it would be important surely. But this is not all. The basic consideration has to do with the removal of all that prevents God from coming to himself in the life of the individual. Whatever there is that blocks this calls for action."

REFLECTION QUESTIONS

- Have you ever had a mystical or unitive experience—a moment when you felt at one with everything? Were such moments a source of fear, or did they draw you closer to God?

- If you are afraid to meet the living presence of God, reflect on why.

- What "kidnaps" your attention and prevents you from taking regular quiet time with God? Consider things like social media, television, overwork, or any intense commitment.

- Has experiencing the presence of God led you toward work in restoring God's beloved creation? If so, how?

SPIRITUAL STEPS

- We can't force mystical encounters, but we can put ourselves in mindsets and places that nurture the possibility of them. Make an appointment with yourself and go to the surroundings that support your own creative encounter with God.

- For a week or more, become an ordinary mystic. Be still and listen for the voice of God at least two or three times or more a day. Try to be open to opportunities to sense the presence of God by taking a contemplative walk or taking a day of silence away from television and electronic devices. Take that sense of Presence with you wherever you go: into meetings, the supermarket, the doctor's office, school, or work.

CHAPTER 8

RESPONSE-ABILITY

UNLEASH INNER AUTHORITY AND SACRED ACTIVISM

If a person knows what word he can use to address you so as to draw you off balance, he can always keep you at his mercy. The basis of inner togetherness, one's sense of inner authority, must never be at the mercy of factors in one's environment, however significant they may be. Nothing from outside a man can destroy him until he opens the door and lets it in. . . . Whatever determines how you feel on the inside controls in large part the destiny of your life.

—Howard Thurman, *Deep Is the Hunger*

During the 1950s in California, my mother consistently displayed what Howard Thurman calls "inner authority." When we ventured into a retail shop like JC Penney or Sears, a salesperson would sometimes address her as "girl." When that happened, Mom would take my hand, turn around, and walk right back out the door.

She taught me to ignore men who thought women were inferior and to deflect verbal attacks that might dampen my aspirations. She showed me how to respond to people who held to certain social conventions about race and gender or presumed I wasn't intelligent because of my skin color. As I got older and began to read about historical figures like Jarena Lee, Zilpha Elaw, Julia Foote, Harriet Jacobs, Sojourner Truth, Harriet Tubman, and more recently Nancy Ambrose, Sue Bailey Thurman, Pauli Murray, and Coretta Scott King, I saw in them the same kind of inner authority I saw in my mother. They shared the same steely resolve to fight for racial and gender equality.

Inner authority is what enabled my mom to turn around and walk back out the door when someone refused to recognize her humanity. Inner authority is what prompted women like Sojourner Truth and Pauli Murray to work for justice. It is what enables us to participate in a social movement or to move away from an abusive relationship. It allows us to accept a call for a vocation or make a decision unpopular with cultural priorities or family dictates.

Howard Thurman's focus on inner authority is life-altering because it leads to a life characterized by inner freedom and purpose. Inner authority carries similar connotations if interpreted from a psychological or spiritual perspective. Noted psychologist Carl Jung described inner authority as the strength that emerges when a person realizes they possess agency. One can act in the world and not be controlled by it. For Thurman, inner authority, as an innate quality, releases us from mental subjugation and dominance. If another person's words and actions disrupt our peace or composure, they possess the power. We enable them to prevail over our inner life and sense of reality.

Thurman's ideas about inner authority plant the seeds for another form of inner authority: one grounded in Spirit. Rooted in a "knowingness" or whispered guidance from Spirit, this type of inner authority unleashes the tenacious courage, vitality, and vision needed for sacred activism. A deep and penetrating examination of our lives is crucial to recognizing inner authority and transforming it into the Spirit-led kind: Inner Authority.

UNVEILING INNER AUTHORITY

Howard Thurman devotes the first segment of the book *Meditations of the Heart* to the discovery of and connection with the presence of God within. In the meditation "The Inward Sea" (which is also the title of the larger section of the book), Thurman makes a series of stunning declarations about inner authority and our awareness of Presence.

The Inward Sea

There is in every person an inward sea, and in that sea there is an island and on that island there is an altar and standing guard before that altar is the "angel with the flaming sword." Nothing can get by that angel to be placed upon that altar unless it has the mark of your inner authority. Nothing passes "the angel with the flaming sword" to be placed upon your altar unless it be a part of "the fluid area of your consent." This is your crucial link with the Eternal.

In this brief meditation, painted with rich spiritual imagery, Thurman speaks to the intrinsic holiness in each of us. The meditation contains a number of probing inquiries. Is there within each of us an inward sea with an island and an altar? An angel with a flaming sword? Do we truly possess the inner authority to determine what is placed on our altar? And what is this "fluid area" of consent? If we believe ourselves to be in command of our lives, reading this meditation may prompt an unsettling feeling. If we are willing to consider that God is omnipresent and resides within us, we can begin to traverse the inward sea and experience our link to God, or the Eternal. Realizing we have never been disconnected from the Presence, we discover a God-created self that does not capitulate to coercion and provocation.

The angel with the flaming sword echoes a reference in the Bible: the cherub with the flaming sword that God placed in the garden of Eden to prevent Adam and Eve from returning (Genesis 3:24). Here Thurman evokes, too, a vision of George Fox on Pendle Hill in England, which involves a tussle with the angel with the flaming sword. Once Fox survived the confrontation, he emerged as a new, radiant self. "A new self emerges and that new self becomes the center of the orientation of my life," Thurman observes in a sermon. "Love does that for us, for it inspires in an individual what was sleeping, relaxed sense of worth and value and meaning, and when this slumbering thing awakens, the kind of radiance that circulates through all the corridors of one's life makes the individual see in himself what he had never seen before. It is the discovery of a new center around which increasingly all of the details of life are more and more organized."

We become aware of our inner authority the moment we recognize our ability to redefine our self-concept. The self-concept—who we think we are—results from messages our families, communities, schools, books, peers, and media convey to us as well as our abilities or competence. Typically this false self, constructed by others, does not resonate with our internal sense of self. The false self does not reflect our passions or dreams, our yearnings or true vocations. Exercising inner authority gives us the resolve to reject false characterizations or prescribed roles. Many people fail to understand that whoever controls their minds dominates them and their lives.

Summoning this power is not as easy as dismissing negative comments. One reason Thurman found segregation, a physical and social structural expression of white supremacy, such an insidious evil is that it attempted to reinforce a sense of unworthiness in Black people by restricting their movement and access to educational and job opportunities. Its design was based on the false assumption that enslaved people lacked the inner life—where dreams, aspirations, desires, and holy callings dwell—that resides in all human beings. But the corrosive effects applied to both sides. Thurman speaks of the toxicity of this form of white supremacy for whites: "But whether the acceptance is delib-erate or indifferent, he becomes the party to a monstrous evil executed in his name and maintained in his behalf. The responsibility for the social decay and the defiling of the spirit is inescapable, acknowledged or unacknowledged. For segregation is a sickness and no one who lives in its reach can claim or expect immunity. It makes men dishonest by forcing them to call an evil thing good; it makes them dis-courteous and rude when it is contrary to their tempera-ment and sense of values to be so."

Wrestling with the angel with the flaming sword may also involve confronting our demons: dishonesty, selfish-ness, addictions, pretensions, or abusive behavior toward ourselves and others. While struggling with these demons, we are able to maintain a holy and sacred space where we meet the presence of God without interference or the dis-tractions that draw our attention away from sacred unity. Reflecting on this same passage, spiritual teacher and activ-ist Barbara Holmes writes, "This island is a bastion of inte-riority, a safe space to encounter God. External oppression may defeat the body and perhaps even the mind, but the inner sanctum will not be breached without consent."

In *Jesus and the Disinherited*, Thurman aptly spotlights Jesus as he directs the emphasis in his teaching to the "inward center" of his followers. Jesus taught that no matter how repressive external circumstances become, as children of God, we are each created with an inner sanctuary—and we need to protect it. Katie Cannon, in her groundbreaking book *Black Womanist Ethics*, writes, "Each person's life must be defined, nurtured and transformed, wherein the self is actualized, affirming the inward authority which arouses greater meaning and potential with each mystical experience." Consistent contact with the presence of God neutralizes verbal and psychological attacks. Thurman reminds us in "The Inward Sea" to align ourselves with the Eternal so that our inward center is fortified.

So how do we discover or strengthen our inner authority? What circumstances in our daily lives require that we exercise inner authority? What obstacles must we remove to connect to our inner authority?

ORIGINS AND USE OF INNER AUTHORITY IN THE LIFE OF HOWARD THURMAN

Nancy Ambrose, Thurman's grandmother, modeled inner authority for him. When her pastor refused to preach and hold the funeral for her son-in-law, Howard's father, Grandma Nancy marched down to the church and held a discussion with the all-male deacon board. Several years later, the deacons rejected Howard's conversion story, which was a requirement for acceptance into the church. Grandma Nancy once again stood up to the deacons, returning with Howard and persuading the men to overturn their decision. With her inner authority on display, Grandma Nancy was highly respected, and people looked to her for courage and counsel. She had internalized the belief that she was a holy child of God. Her deep and abiding spirituality and radical trust in God became central to her self-concept, and she desired the same for her grandson. "She acted as one who had inner authority," writes Luther Smith Jr. "Rather than being controlled by her environment, she exercised control over it."

Thurman would return to this theme as he dissected the Gospels. He felt that Jesus outlined the way for every person to be released from psychological bondage by claiming his or her identity as a holy child of God.

As Thurman matured, his own inner authority repeatedly became apparent. Thurman modeled inner authority when he resigned from a tenured position—as professor and dean of the Rankin Chapel at Howard University—to start a new church in San Francisco. Initially he had no idea how he would support his family, but his commitment to create the first intentionally interracial and interdenominational church emerged from a deep yearning that he believed shaped his destiny. The entire endeavor seemed nonsensical and selfish to many colleagues and friends. By leaving Howard University, his friends said, he would be denying Negro students—many of them future religious leaders—access to his great knowledge and wisdom.

Thurman also drew strong criticism for his lack of active participation in the civil rights movement. Through his inner authority and commentary on the inner life, we learn the reasons and history behind his decision. He *knew* he was not an organizer or tactician. He recognized at a deep level that he was not called to be a Martin Luther King Jr. Instead, Thurman was called to be a spiritual architect and guide, someone who could be a companion to many of the movement's prominent leaders. "It was my discovery that more than campaigns or propaganda, however efficacious for creating the climate for social change, my gifts moved in the direction of motivation of the individual and what could be done by the individual in his home, in his life, on his street," he said. Thurman felt political activism would detract from his ability to serve as a spiritual director or companion for others. "I didn't have to wait for the revolution," he told one interviewer. "I have never been in search for identity—I think that [all] I've ever felt and worked on and believed in was founded in a kind of private, almost unconscious autonomy that did not seek vindication in my environment because it was in me." Thurman chose not to cede his inner authority to critics or supporters but instead to heed the sound of the genuine in his own spirit.

So often we look out at the world with so many problems—disasters, famines, suffering, war—and we feel overwhelmed. Where do we begin, and will we ever be done? We get stuck trying to answer every call for help. Learning to exercise inner authority allows us to say no to some invitations for action and to discern which ones call out for our yes.

INNER LIFE

People who listened to or encountered him often sensed a certain intimacy with Thurman. His charisma stemmed in part from the way he exposed his inner life. "In speaking and writing, he discloses the struggles, pain, humor, embarrassments, despair, and hope of his life," writes Luther

Smith Jr. about this way that Thurman had of baring his soul. People knew they could trust him because he revealed his own ambivalences and contradictions. His willingness to share himself in this way gave others a chance to join him in an experience of God, writes Smith.

Thurman knew that a familiarity with one's inner life is a basic requirement of spiritual formation. By becoming acquainted with and operating from our own inward center, we are less subject to volatility or impermanence. If we choose this courageous work, the benefits are akin to the fruit of the Spirit. Here is where inner transformation morphs into the foundation for sacred calls.

Thurman confirms the emphasis on spirituality as necessary for social change.

"The quality of the inner life is primary," he writes. "An accurate sense of self is necessary if one is to transform the social order into a community. This accuracy is only possible if the individual is rooted in and committed to the spiritual life." And Thurman delves further into the links between inner life and what he labels "world-mindedness." All our desires, ideas about who we are, attitudes and values, and even ruminations about the world constitute our inner narrative. "The inner life, therefore, is activity that takes place within consciousness but does not originate there and is a part of a reality central to all of life and is at once the ground of all awareness, of all aliveness," he writes. "It is here that man becomes conscious of his meaning and his destiny as a child, an offspring of God." An exploration of our inner world gives us an indication of how we view and operate in the outer world.

World-mindedness, in Thurman's words, "places at the center of all political, social, or economic arrangements . . . a profound recognition of basic solidarity and concern for the guaranteeing of the right of each individual to have a climate in which his life may unfold in dignity, beauty, and fullness." As we examine our inner lives, we must consider the impact of our personal decisions on other people. Our lives are intertwined like fibers spun into woven fabric.

For some, the inner life may remain like an unread mystery novel left on a bookshelf. Lisa Colón DeLay uses the analogy of "flyover territory" to describe the segments of ourselves we may never delve into. "My inner world has unknown terrain, and so does yours," writes DeLay. "This expanse includes our minds, hearts, wills, and spirits. The wild land within also includes our experiences, aspirations, and memories. And like it or not, this territory also includes shadowy areas of hidden influences as well as triggering thoughts and feelings. . . . We all, at times, avoid looking at painful or difficult parts of our inner selves because of our fears or the commotion of our lives. Some people manage to avert their gaze from their interior terrains for a lifetime."

INNER AUTHORITY

Navigating our interiority allows for the emergence of inner authority and readies the spirit for Spirit, what I'll call "Inner Authority." Inner Authority does not emerge from us but from Spirit within—what Thurman labels "the Eternal." Fr. Richard Rohr describes it as wisdom springing forth like a water fountain from the Indwelling Spirit. In an interview,

Rohr distinguishes between external authorities and Inner Authority. "By relying on Absolute Authority such as the Pope for Catholics and the Bible for Protestants, what got eliminated from the conversation was Inner Authority," comments Rohr. "The indwelling Holy Spirit is the basis for Inner Authority. It is not in opposition to scriptural authority or church authority but when they regulate and balance one another, you tend to have very solid and creative people. . . . The Indwelling Spirit was meant to localize that dignity inherently in each person."

Rohr uses the three wheels of a tricycle as a metaphor for different kinds of authority—scripture, tradition, and experience—and asks us to envision the Indwelling Holy Spirit as the driver of the tricycle.

Inner Authority is key for sustaining sacred activism. When we pause, ask for guidance, and follow it, we move with a power undergirded by the Spirit of God. "Thurman was inspired, convicted, and taught by the truth which came through him. His own life served as a fundamental authority for wisdom and faith," writes Luther Smith Jr. Thurman further illuminates this aspect of Inner Authority in his meditation "The Strength to Be Free." "It takes strength to affirm the high prerogative of your spirit. And you will find that if you do, a host of invisible angels will wing to your defense, and the glory of the living God will envelop your surroundings because in you He has come into His own."

Inner Authority is another way to live from Spirit and to connect with an authentic or spiritual self, the one God created. It is essential for healing all people, whether they are victims of oppression or perpetrators of it.

DISCERNMENT AS THE MISSING LINK

Vital to the exercise of Inner Authority is the practice of discernment. Discernment is the spiritual practice of decision-making by which we bring decisions into prayer. Spiritual leader Rose Mary Dougherty notes, "The eye of the heart grows accustomed to recognizing, almost spontaneously, those (interior) movements that are drawing us into oneness with ourselves and all creation in God and those that tend to isolate us even from ourselves." Discerning with Spirit operates in contrast to our contemporary inclination to just figure things out or make decisions based on accrual of wealth and status and success. Unfortunately, many people remain unaware or neglect to access this abiding Inner Wisdom.

Quaker mystic Thomas Kelly portrays discernment as a contemplative stance—a "simplification" of all the warring obligations, compulsions, and activities competing for our attention. To drop down into a holy center where we surrender to God is to know our true selves. This description mirrors Thurman's adage of yielding one's "nerve center" to God. Discernment facilitates self-knowledge, as it illuminates who we truly are. Kelly encourages us to release our worldly attachments or affiliations and, in Thurman's words, "follow the grain of your own wood" or "do what makes you come alive."

Kelly recommends we move slowly as we prune away all that does not feed our authentic selves. The more authentic we are, the stronger and more available we are to move with Inner Authority to our sacred calling. We cultivate Inner Authority by giving small or large decisions to Spirit and waiting patiently for an answer. Some practitioners of discernment ask for a clear sign or an undeniable indication of a leading.

Thurman relates how, before accepting a position at Boston University, initially he prayed but didn't receive any guidance. Contacted several times by the then president of Boston University, Harold Case, about his decision, Thurman gently and firmly explained that he simply didn't have an answer. He could not move until he received a "word in his heart." In this way, he discerned a way forward by waiting for Inner Authority. The practice of discernment is not asking God for permission. It simply allows holy wisdom to permeate our babbling minds.

Thurman desired to improve the plight of his people; he wanted them to have freedom and full citizenship and longed for every human spirit to actualize their full potential. But he yearned for healing and unity as well. Thurman saw the connection between the two—personal fulfillment and community. Union with God required both.

WALKING WITH INNER AUTHORITY TOWARD SACRED ACTIVISM

The popularity of the term "sacred activism" has mushroomed in recent years. But in addition to defining sacred activism for our era, it's important to remember the witness of sacred activists throughout history. More than sixty years ago, when Thurman linked living from the presence of God to his sacred call, he joined a longstanding community of sacred activists. They consist of people like Moses, Jesus, Joan of Arc, George Fox, Sojourner Truth, Harriet Tubman, Mahatma Gandhi, Olive Schreiner, Martin Luther King Jr., Fannie Lou Hamer, Rev. Otis T. Moss II, Muriel Lester, and unknown numbers of foot soldiers in many domestic and international movements. In contemporary times, we might include in a roster of sacred activists Rev. William Barber II, Rev. Otis T. Moss III, Barbara Holmes, Jim Wallis, Rev. Jacqui Lewis, Adam Bucko, Mathew Fox, Andrew Harvey, Francisco "Pancho" Ramos Stierle, and thousands more.

Sacred activists are those who invite Spirit's guidance about *how to take action, when to take action, what to say*, and *when to say it.* Discerning answers to these questions gives a sacred dimension to social change and justice work. A certain holiness prevails when we choose to collaborate with Spirit in seeking humanity and unity for every part of God's beloved creation.

Jarena Lee, Zilpha Elaw, and Julia Foote were three courageous and Spirit-led Black women of the nineteenth century who heard a call from Spirit to preach. Their autobiographies are featured in the lovely book *Sisters of the Spirit*, edited by William L. Andrews. Lee, after years of internal conflict about her salvation, and relieved that her soul had been finally sanctified, heard a voice one day during a silent moment. She writes, "there seemed to sound a voice which

I distinctly heard, and most certainly understood, which said to me, 'Go preach the Gospel!' I immediately replied aloud, 'No one will believe me.' Again I listened, and again the same voice seemed to say, 'Preach the Gospel; I will put words in your mouth, and will turn your enemies to become your friends.'" After the voice, Lee prayed to the Lord to make certain the voice came from Spirit and not from Satan. Suddenly a vision of a Bible and pulpit appeared in front of her as she kneeled.

Religious dictates at the time did not permit women to preach from the pulpit, but Lee began to preach in homes and meetinghouses and to any gatherings that would receive her. All three of these women used Inner Authority to defy local conventions. They preached and offered pastoral care throughout their regions and even overseas.

We see evidence of Inner Authority in Martin Luther King Jr., who one day knelt down on the Edmund Pettus Bridge, paused, prayerfully listened—and decided to turn around the marchers. He sensed that it wasn't time yet. Harriet Tubman invoked Inner Authority each time she made a move—asking Spirit about which routes to take, the best times to travel, and who she could trust to secure freedom for herself and others. To live a life rooted in God, to listen without ceasing for promptings and direction from Spirit: these result in an Inner Authority that cannot be usurped because God is the force behind the movement.

It takes humility, inner freedom, and vitality to acknowledge and use Inner Authority, to accept one's sacred call even though it may not be of your choosing. Each of us becomes a sacred activist when we accept our call, even if it is in our households or faith communities or on the job.

Howard Thurman represents a prototype for sacred activism because he used his inner authority and Inner Authority to create a spiritual roadmap for the civil rights movement and the nonviolent direct-action campaigns that preceded it. His life became a spiritual refuge for activists. He held the spiritual space for many of its participants and promoted a living wisdom that continues to feed us more than forty years after his death.

Howard Thurman focused on personal spiritual renewal because social transformation involves much more than a change in the laws or political climate. For internal freedom to come from the oppressed themselves, says Luther Smith Jr., summarizing Thurman, "There must be a change in their response-ability against the oppressive factors. This response-ability is largely an internal transformation where the oppressed realize a new status which redefines their worth and power. They come to attain a proper sense of self."

The longevity and impact of the civil rights movement inspired social justice work in many domains throughout the world. The task of spiritual and social transformation continues, as each new generation births new prophets and sacred activists.

REFLECTION QUESTIONS

- Who are your models of inner authority? What about of Inner Authority (inner authority that is grounded in the Indwelling Spirit)?

- Can you think of times when you relied on your inner authority or Inner Authority?

- How familiar are you with your inner life? How would you describe it—its quality and its ambience?

- How have you practiced discernment around decision-making?

- Do you feel like you know what you are called to do? If so, what form of sacred activism has Spirit called you to? If not, what are the questions that come to mind?

SPIRITUAL STEPS

- Pause and ask Spirit about a small or large decision. Listen and pay attention to how and when the answer may appear.

- Take an unscheduled day and spend it following your Inner Authority. Ask Spirit for guidance about everything you do throughout the day, including what and when to eat. Make this a regular weekly or monthly spiritual practice.

- If you are following your sacred calling, find ways to help others discover theirs. Organize a group or host a gathering.

CHAPTER 9

FULL CIRCLE

ENGAGE IN SPIRITUAL MENTORING

There are many of us ... across the world who claim Howard
Thurman as a personal spiritual mentor. He spoke to our condition
as no one else did. He inspired, challenged, lifted, and comforted us
in a thousand ways. His words on a printed page, in certain lines
and passages, we read with recognition that he was communicat-
ing directly with us—vividly, intensely, personally. In the stillness
of a quiet room many of us have sat alone, or with a friend, and
listened to his voice on tape, and experienced the touching of our
mind by his mind, our spirit by his spirit. Or we have been in a
church, or a lecture hall, or a classroom and watched him labor
and struggle to bring forth just the right word with just the right
message that deepened our understanding and raised our vision.
—Landrum Bolling, quoted in *Howard Thurman: His*
Enduring Dream

The melodious voice of Howard Thurman bellows through
the room: "How good it is to center down," he says. His

voice is filled with gravity, but it is not without a sense of joy. It has an almost incantatory quality, a cadence both warm and mysterious. Each time I play a recording of Thurman reciting one of his many meditations, I smile. Like Landrum Bolling writes, many of us feel like Thurman speaks directly to us—"vividly, intensely, personally."

Once I started reading and listening to Thurman, I stopped feeling strange for seeking silence, stillness, and solitude. My awkwardness as the only African American on a silent retreat or at a spiritual conference dissipated. In him I found support for my desire for intimacy with God and hunger for spiritual community, and I began to consider him a mentor.

Thurman personally mentored and inspired many social and political activists, among them Pauli Murray, James Farmer, Bayard Rustin, James Lawson, Dr. Martin Luther King Jr., Jesse Jackson, Marian Wright Edelman, Vernon Jordan, and Vincent Harding. Legions of individuals— faculty, staff, and students at Spelman College, Morehouse College, Howard University, and Boston University; members of the Church for the Fellowship of All Peoples; those in attendance at Sunday worship at Marsh Chapel; and the readers of his books and listeners of his catalogued lectures and sermons—have absorbed his quiet and determined direction. Something in his rich, poetic voice and profound wisdom speaks to the deeper places within us.

Being mentored by Thurman or someone else, however, does not mean we simply stop there. As those who have been mentored, we are called into mentoring others.

THURMAN'S MENTORS

Born into a community of trusted guides, Howard Thurman understood the importance of having a spiritual mentor and, eventually, of being one for others. "For Thurman, real learning always required the intimacy and intensity of personal mentoring," write Quinton Dixie and Peter Eisenstadt. "He had always sought out teachers who could provide this, and he would try to be that sort of teacher himself, giving several generations of students the same sort of close spiritual encounters that had been so important to him." Howard Thurman needed spiritual mentors to reach the apex of his potential, and he blossomed into his role as mentor. Prominent people dotted young Thurman's surroundings, including the family physician, John Stocking, and renowned educator and activist Mary McLeod Bethune. Yet his grandmother Nancy Ambrose, Mordecai Wyatt Johnson, George Cross, and Rufus Jones served as his chief mentors. Let's look at how these individuals molded and shaped him and his thinking.

GRANDMA NANCY

Grandma Nancy served as Howard Thurman's first mentor. She pushed him to develop his mind and live from his spirit. A close friend of Thurman's, George Makechnie, notes, "Grandmother Nancy was Howard's rock. Her spiritual strength, wisdom, and good sense had a profound influence upon his growth, shaping, and development." Makechnie highlights, as Thurman himself did, the way he would read to her from scripture. I imagine him sitting beside her, how proud he must have felt, how precious were these moments he shared with her. She could not read, Makechnie writes, but "she firmly believed an education was of primary importance, and especially so to Blacks. 'Your only chance,' she told Howard, 'is to get an education. The white man will destroy you if you don't.'"

A tale about Grandma Nancy's redemptive love demonstrates something of what she modeled for Howard. The story circulates today in sermons and lectures, although it's hard to know whether it actually happened. Still, the story holds value for what it evokes of Grandma Nancy's character. When Howard was a child, a white woman who lived adjacent to their home apparently resented having Black people live near her. Each night she dumped chicken manure she had scraped from her chicken coop over the fence onto Grandma Nancy's garden. Young Howard wondered why his grandmother did not become enraged at her neighbor's hateful act and exact some sort of revenge. Grandma Nancy chose instead to rise early and mix the manure into the soil and use it as fertilizer. This practice continued for years.

One day the old white woman, who lived alone, became ill. Being an authentic Christian, Grandma Nancy stopped by her neighbor's house with some chicken soup and a bouquet of roses. The woman was deeply moved by Grandma Nancy's acts of kindness and asked her where she had found the beautiful long-stem red roses. Grandma Nancy Ambrose told the neighbor that she herself had played a role in growing the beautiful roses. She reminded her about the chicken manure she had dumped regularly in her backyard.

The God Grandma Nancy worshipped showed her how to turn hate into love. Thurman espouses this form of redemptive love in *Jesus and the Disinherited*, in which he reminds his readers that Jesus treated people not in proportion to who they were but to who they could be. Thurman knew that healing a fractured nation would require this type of transformational love.

MORDECAI WYATT JOHNSON

While attending the Florida Baptist Academy, Thurman joined the Young Men's Christian Association (YMCA). Although highly segregated, the YMCA created programs for the uplift of boys and young men. His election as president of his local chapter during his sophomore year allowed Thurman to attend his first King's Mountain conference where he heard the great orator Mordecai Wyatt Johnson. Johnson had served as a former student secretary of the International YMCA Committee. Howard was so impressed and stirred by Johnson's message that he wrote him a letter. Despite his earlier ambivalence about the church, due to how it scorned his father's death, Howard pleaded with Johnson to become his mentor. "I want to be a minister of the Gospel. I feel the needs of my people, I see their distressing condition, and have offered myself upon the altar as a living sacrifice, in order that I may help the 'skinned and flung down' as you interpret. God wants me and His precious love urges me to take up the cross and follow Him," wrote the young Howard.

Johnson wrote back, and they continued their correspondence and personal relationship for many years. Possibly the most important piece of wisdom that Thurman incorporated into his adult life came from Johnson. He told Howard, "Keep in close touch with your people, especially with those who need your service. Take every opportunity to encourage their growth and to serve them. School yourself to think over all that you learn, in relation to them and to their needs. Make yourself believe that the humblest, most ignorant and most backward of them is worthy of the best prepared thought in life that you can give." Howard Thurman took this wisdom into his spirit, and it directed him throughout his life.

GEORGE CROSS

As a student at Rochester Theological Seminary, Howard Thurman took several courses taught by George Cross. He also had private conferences with him and was advised by him. Thurman wrote that Cross "had a greater influence on my life than any other person who ever lived. Everything about me was alive when I came into his presence." In their personal meetings, held frequently on Saturday mornings in Cross's faculty office, Thurman bantered with Cross, asking questions and making challenges. Cross would listen with great patience, Thurman later wrote, and then would "reduce my arguments to ash."

George Cross believed in the brilliance of Howard Thurman, but as we saw earlier, he could not grasp the reality of racism, nor the extent to which it tries to annihilate unrealized potential in its victims.

RUFUS JONES

As an instructor and mentor, Rufus Jones helped Thurman refine his thinking about the links between mysticism and social transformation. They spent many hours discussing how the inward life is connected to outward experience and how mysticism might expand efforts to remedy international conflict and poverty. Although they did not discuss race, which Thurman viewed as a blind spot in Jones's analysis, Thurman knew he could use mysticism to alleviate the plight of Negroes. His intense kinship with Jones only deepened his intellectual grasp and personal experience of mysticism.

In June 1929, Howard Thurman wrote a note to Rufus Jones thanking him for "the huge share which you have had in the enrichment of my life during the past five months. I cannot now estimate the significance of the days with you at Haverford." As a result of Thurman's work on mysticism or religious experience, spiritual seekers and sacred activists continue to reap the benefits of this unique mentoring relationship.

Thurman carried the lessons and words of these spiritual mentors with him in his mind and in his heart. They would become models for him as he, too, became a mentor for others.

MENTORING OTHERS

Howard Thurman serves as an exemplar for both the formal ministry of spiritual direction and informal spiritual friendship. Mentoring, at its best, is an exchange. Spiritual guides are vital beacons of light on the spiritual path, and once a person becomes spiritually mature, they naturally begin to serve as spiritual mentors for others. Maya Angelou instructs, "When you learn, teach." Howard Thurman taught and mentored many, although not always in a formal classroom. Students found they could share their personal issues with Thurman and frequently sought him out for spiritual advice. His timeless sermons, public lectures, and written meditations endure because they continue to feed the hunger of the spirit. Let's look at a few of the people he mentored.

MARTIN LUTHER KING JR.

We've already seen how Howard Thurman's indelible mark on the American civil rights movement runs directly through his influence on Martin Luther King Jr. Clearly, the respect went both ways. Thurman expresses his great admiration for King with these words:

> As a result of a series of fortuitous consequences there appeared on the horizon of the common life a young man who for a swift, staggering, and startling moment met the demands of the hero. He was young. He was well-educated with the full credentials of

academic excellence in accordance with ideals found in white society. He was a son of the South. He was steeped in and nurtured by familiar religious tradition. He had charisma, that intangible quality of personality that gathers up in its magic the power to lift people out of themselves without diminishing them. In him the "outsider" and the "insider" came together in a triumphant synthesis. Here at last was a man who affirmed the oneness of black and white under a transcendent unity, for whom community meant the profoundest sharing in the common life. For him, the wall was a temporary separation between brothers. And his name was Martin Luther King Jr.

Religious scholar Paul Harvey says, "Thurman was a private man and an intellectual; he was not an activist, as King was, nor one to take a specific social and political cause to transform a country. But he mentored an entire generation, including King, who did just that. Thurman's lesson to King was that the cultivation of the self feeds and enriches the struggle for social justice. In a larger sense, the discipline of nonviolence required a spiritual commitment and discipline that came, for many, through self-examination, meditation, and prayer." Thurman transmitted that message to the larger civil rights movement.

It was at Crozier Seminary where Martin Luther King took a class from George Washington Davis, one of Thurman's classmates at Rochester Seminary, and also read and wrote about Thurman's seminal work *Jesus and the Disinherited.*

King would later incorporate some of Thurman's notions into some of his own writings and speeches. Although King did not consider himself a mystic, he was moved and amazed by the mystical wisdom of Thurman. Howard and Sue Bailey Thurman expressed hope that King would consider becoming the pastor of Fellowship Church, but King felt called to Montgomery to begin active work in the civil rights movement. Working behind the scenes, Howard Thurman became his spiritual adviser.

One story illustrates their spiritual connection. In 1958, a mentally disturbed woman attempted to assassinate Martin Luther King Jr. by stabbing him. Thurman writes that he experienced a "visitation," or vision, and knew he needed to travel to New York to speak with King.

Thurman found King at Harlem Hospital and strongly urged him to take a much longer recuperation period and to include some time for silence and solitude. He needed to assess his role in the movement, in a venture that had taken on a life of its own. King later wrote to Thurman about how their meeting had been "a spiritual uplift, and of inestimable value in giving me the strength and courage to face the future of that trying period." Historian Taylor Branch points out that this time was a period of relative quiet for King, a unique season within the rest of his adult life. There were no talks or lectures, but just solitude. It was after this respite that King took a five-week trip to India, studied the principles of nonviolence and civil disobedience, and laid a wreath at the grave of Mahatma Gandhi.

The ideas about a nonviolent religion and Jesus as a nonviolent liberator that Thurman developed in the years before and during his tenure at Fellowship Church received a larger audience through the publication of *Jesus and the Disinherited* in 1949. This book deeply influenced other leaders of the civil rights struggle. Thurman offered the vision of spiritual discipline that informed the moral basis of the Black freedom movement in the South. During these years, while serving on the boards of Fellowship for Reconciliation (FOR) and Congress of Racial Equality CORE, he spoke with leaders of these organizations and others—including Bayard Rustin, James Lawson, Vernon Jordan, James Farmer, Pauli Murray, Jesse Jackson, and Whitney Young—about matters both political and spiritual. But Thurman always preferred offering quiet counsel and private intellectual guidance to garnering political visibility. His influence would extend into the future to touch the lives of many religious scholars and scores of spiritual seekers, including Alice Walker and Barack Obama.

MARIAN WRIGHT EDELMAN

Like a river, Howard Thurman's sway flowed along several tributaries, inspiring women and men who chose to devote their lives to important yet sometimes less visible causes. Marian Wright Edelman, founder and president emerita of the Children's Defense Fund, found kinship with Thurman in the ways in which they were reared. They both emerged from families of deep faith who worked to buffer them from the hostile worlds they would encounter. Edelman writes, "Still, as in the days of Thurman's childhood and in the day of my childhood, countless children in these most difficult, unjust, undeserved circumstances are bolstered and strengthened, nurtured and protected by parents, and others who struggle to counter the world's message and remind their children that they are sacred gifts from God and precious in God's sight." Her parents, like Thurman's grandmother and mother, didn't want her to internalize negative and damaging social messages. Their loving protection gave her a certain inner strength that enabled her to take her prophetic message about the care of children into adulthood.

Edelman first encountered the words of Howard Thurman as a young girl exploring the books in her minister father's study. Then as a college student, she heard Thurman speak when he visited Spelman Chapel. What kept her grounded in her work to save and support children, Edelman writes, were the urgings to pray, meditate, reflect, and be thankful for grace. In the centering moment, we find a "breath of renewal, and a recognition that we can only do our most faithful best and then turn it over to God. We cannot sustain this work if we are not centered." Edelman took in Thurman's words like a holy communion. Meditations of his like "Remember the Children" inspired her to hold "the big hope that never quite deserts me" and to continue in her struggles to end violence, promote love, and protect innocent children from needless suffering.

VINCENT HARDING

The deep waters of Howard Thurman's wisdom also touched historian, educator, theologian, and activist Vincent Harding, who considered Thurman a surrogate father. Like so many others, Harding first met Thurman on the pages of *Jesus and the Disinherited*, which he read as a graduate student at the University of Chicago. Many years later, after the assassination of Martin Luther King Jr., a close and personal relationship burgeoned between these two great men. Thurman offered solace, care, and guidance in what Harding describes as the gloomy days following King's death. During many long walks up the steep and winding streets of San Francisco, Harding and Thurman laughed and talked. Thurman invited Harding and his wife, Rosemarie Freeney Harding, to join him and Sue in their home for relaxation and fellowship.

Harding understood that Howard Thurman occupied the important role of mentor and companion to those summoned to the streets to march. As nonviolent demonstrators prepared for action, and when they returned victorious or defeated, Harding writes, "Thurman offered clarification, hope, and encouragement." Thurman would sit with civil rights demonstrators and listen and pose questions rather than issue commands. He would ask them about what they were seeking and why and what means they utilized to achieve their goals. As a spiritual mentor, Thurman conveyed to them his firm belief that there could be no defeat of the movement if their motives remained oriented toward the oneness.

"I remember going to him in times of deep personal need, occasionally talking by phone, sometimes face to face," Harding recalls. "He was always solidly present, listening, understanding, admonishing when necessary, sharing silence, surrounding and undergirding me with prayers, doing whatever else seemed helpful. We could feel Howard and Sue keeping our entire family and a special place of love and meditation between them. I remember our silences. They were filled with his wisdom and compassion. Indeed, it may be that he was the wisest and most compassionate man I have ever known."

FULL CIRCLE

The wisdom of life exists to be passed on so that others will not suffer needlessly. A gifted mentor like Howard Thurman spurred people to refine who they already were and to recognize the strengths and talents they possess. Relying on some of Thurman's words, noted author Sam Keen shares how Howard Thurman encouraged him to find his own vision: "Follow the grain in your own wood."

Peter Eisenstadt observes, "Throughout his career, Thurman was in demand as a mentor and advisor. Counseling is, of course, a core responsibility for all members of the clergy, but Thurman clearly had a special calling for it, less a matter of dispensing advice than assuming the role of a spiritual psychologist, to help others to find their inner voice, what he later called 'sound of the genuine,' and to assist them in formulating and answering their own questions."

One of the joys of being a professor for me was advising and mentoring students. I nudged them to try different forms of mindfulness, including meditation, to prevent test anxiety, spark creativity, and prompt innovative thinking. I highlighted the importance of retreats, especially silent ones, to re-energize and guard against burnout and stress. I enjoyed sitting and chatting with students, waiting for that special moment when their eyes would brighten and I would observe them "come alive," as Thurman describes.

The answers I have uncovered in the silence, the stillness, the quietness, the pausing, the "resting lull": these answers emanate from the same Source Thurman drew from, the same wisdom that must be shared. He will remain my spiritual guide and companion, as his life and words lead me to the Light, to the Wholeness he knew.

REFLECTION QUESTIONS

- Who have been your formal or informal spiritual mentors? These might include a family member, teacher, minister, author, retreat leader, or church member. What specific wisdom have you garnered from them?

- Who do you serve as spiritual mentor or model for? Who seeks your guidance?

SPIRITUAL STEPS

- We all can spot a wise person. Seek out the sage in your church, synagogue, temple, mosque, school, or job. Arrange for a meal, walk, or conversation.

- Visit with and pursue a mentoring relationship with a relative, neighbor, or wise elder.

- Howard Thurman felt prompted to visit Martin Luther King Jr. after the stabbing. Consider who you might feel prompted to talk with.

- Be intentional about scheduling time to serve as an informal spiritual mentor. Spend some time meditating on this question and then get in touch with someone who has sought you out in the past and offer time for a conversation.

CHAPTER 10

TO LIVE FULLY

WALK THE PATH OF LIBERATING SPIRITUALITY

It is very good to turn aside from the rush and weariness and the
anxieties by which these days beset and lay siege to our moments,
to rest in the presence of God. It is good to pause to make an
end of so much that bothers and harasses the spirit, to assess the
meaning of our lives in the light of the movement of the Spirit
within us.

—Howard Thurman, *The Centering Moment*

Perhaps you have wondered what it would feel like to move
through each day with an awareness of the presence of God.
I have. What would it feel like to give priority to the stir-
rings of Spirit over all the other demands that cause rush,
anxiety, and weariness? Would you climb out of bed in the
morning eager to join the adventure to which you've been
called, trusting that God goes with you?

When we walk through the life and work of Howard Thurman, we see what a grounded spirituality looks like, one in which Spirit guides our steps and prods us to work for unity and oneness. We may not yet know what it feels like, but perhaps we have caught glimpses.

Some of us used to attend to our spiritual selves but have recently ignored them, while others have never fully explored them. Some of us were handed a spirituality by parents or churches that we tried on for a while but that never seemed to fit or even felt damaging. Here we are, more than forty years after Thurman's death, still locked in our private cells of political, social, and religious tribalism and narcissism. Clearly, the infrastructure of our current spirituality is in dire need of repair lest it implode.

So how might we envision a spirituality that forms bridges instead of builds barriers—bridges that we can walk across into community, the common unity that Thurman believed we all share? What structural supports, guardrails, and roads are needed to lead us to an awareness of oneness? What materials will fortify and maintain a reconstructed spirituality?

Thurman lived with inner authority as a mystic and sacred activist, with reverence for the self and for every holy child of God. He issued a call to oneness with all of God's beloved creation and to a liberating spirituality that makes you feel as if you have come alive. Living from the presence of God as he did shifts us from a life centered in the world to one aligned with God. Becoming an ordinary mystic— allowing our religious or mystical experiences or creative encounters to guide us—may involve nothing less than reconstructing our spirituality.

MYSTICISM FOR EVERYDAY LIFE

The loving, living wisdom of Howard Thurman invites us to join with the Source of all life. The presence of God radiates through silence and solitude, nature, sacred synchronicities, and the religion of Jesus. It imbues our creative encounters, Inner Authority, sacred activism, and spiritual mentoring. Mystical moments permit this same Presence to infuse our everyday lives.

We can ignore or deny that we are spiritual beings. But Thurman reminds us that beneath all our ego desires—for importance, fortune, power, and possessions—is a hunger for our Creator. Walking in a fog of forgetfulness, we cannot see that as human spirits, our bond with God is indestructible.

Mozella Mitchell refers to Thurman as a "modern day sophisticated shaman" because he did not attempt to persuade others to embrace his religious or spiritual positions. Instead, Thurman shook loose the sacred in other people. They came away from his talks and sermons moved to ponder their own spiritual natures. By cultivating a mystical consciousness, we, too, can arouse spirituality in others.

Mystics live among us, and they have done so since the beginning of time. Religious scholar Joy Bostic outlines the ecstatic and spiritual practices of African American women in the nineteenth century. The list includes visitations, visions, dreams, contemplative prayer, and meditation, similar to

West African mystical practices. Bostic spotlights the lives of Jarena Lee, Sojourner Truth, and Rebecca Cox Jackson as prototypes for mystic-activists. "The mystical experiences of these women did not cause them to resign themselves to a mystical life of seclusion," Bostic writes. "Rather it motivated, inspired, and empowered them to seek out and work within the community and participate in bringing about a more just vision of local communities within their world." These Black female mystics modeled the activism that ordinary mysticism calls us to. As they followed the guidance of Spirit, they formed a crucial component of the reconstructed spirituality that Thurman proposes.

The process of becoming an ordinary mystic may appear simple: skip from one spiritual practice to another and another until you have an ecstatic experience and feel you have arrived. But eventually most of us stumble upon a boulder on the path: surrender.

As David and I delved more into the mystical experience that he described to me in chapter 7, I asked if he considered himself a mystic. He stammered and hesitated. David wasn't certain he was ready to relinquish that much control—to cede the "nerve center" of his being, as Thurman describes it, to God. Willfulness sometimes hovers beside our willingness. The fear of losing autonomy, or of claiming a unique identity, can terrify even the most devoted seeker. To claim a mystical consciousness means admitting to a mode of seeing and thinking that brings us out of the prayer room into the larger world. It also demands a commitment to God, a trust in the unseen.

In an inner world full of ceaseless chatter and an outer world filled with unrelenting distractions, Thurman firmly but gently nudges us to listen for God. Where does attending to our spiritual life fall on our list of daily tasks? How can we walk forward as ordinary mystics? Setting God as the priority in everything we do, in every decision we make, may become a lifelong pursuit.

LIBERATING SPIRITUALITY

Simply rearranging our spiritual lives for the sake of novelty or trend is not the way forward. A restructured spirituality must be liberating. In the foreword of the 1996 edition of *Jesus of the Disinherited*, Vincent Harding describes Thurman as offering a liberating spirituality that unchains the spirit so that a person is free to live out his or her own call. Those who become freed from damaging beliefs—of being cursed or unworthy from birth or somehow deserving of their disinherited state—could work to free others: those who are yet to realize they are unfree, as well as their oppressors. Harding remembers Thurman's words: "Our dreams will not rest until they incarnate themselves in us, in each of us, in all of us for all of us."

Harding suggests that a liberating spirituality is both rooted and reaching out—like a tree. In a 1998 address titled "Dangerous Spirituality," given at Rankin Chapel at Howard University, Harding shared his perspective on the spirituality of Howard Thurman and Martin Luther King Jr. A liberating spirituality is always seeking because there is always more to learn, to know. "The spirituality of Howard Thurman was that of a seeker who sought for healing of his people and of his nation," Harding says. A spirituality that moved in and through horrifying experiences anchored both Thurman and King. They struggled to move the United States toward its promise of democracy and individuals toward the oneness God intended. Harding admits that to hold such a nondual position is challenging.

But a liberating spirituality demands spiritual resiliency. The Black people who surrounded me when I was growing up demonstrated intense perseverance and resolve. Anytime I faced a setback at school or at work, family and friends reminded me to get up and try again. Determination was a part of my racial and cultural history. God would make a way, but I had to crawl if I wanted to rise again.

Pauli Murray describes spiritual resiliency as a necessary part of the struggle. As she studied economic oppression around the world in the 1940s, she noted that Negroes held an honorable place in history for their spiritual resiliency. They were forever pushing, from the time of enslavement onward, for their humanity. This vital history gave her the strength and courage to keep the faith. "Seeing the relationship between my personal cause and the universal cause of freedom released me from a sense of isolation, helped me to rid myself of vestiges of shame over my racial history, and gave me an unequivocal understanding that equality of treatment was my birthright and not something to be earned," Murray writes. "I would be no less afraid to challenge the system of racial segregation, but the heightened significance of my cause would impel me to act in spite of my fears."

Something about feeling the fear and fighting for freedom anyway helped Pauli Murray and others to break out of the prison of dehumanization. This growing awakening of the sanctity of one's self is the spark that Thurman desired to ignite in the minds and actions of young people. He imagined a volcano of spiritual energy removing every impediment to the full expression of an authentic self.

Although we tend to focus on Thurman's impact on unleashing the inner and outer freedom of the disinherited, he understood that members of the dominant groups needed to be liberated too. Thurman recognized that the damaging effects of oppression include the spiritual contamination of both victim and perpetrator, sufferer and offender. Pauli Murray shares a story about a young white male autoworker from Georgia, called Red, who studied as she did at the Brookwood Labor College. For the first time, he was forced to live and interact with Black people as equals. "I suspected that he had bolstered his self-esteem through a blind belief in the superiority of skin color and that his fragile security was shattered when he was forced to recognize that there were Negroes who had achieved a superior education in spite of barriers," Murray reflects. "I felt sorry for Red, and for the first time saw clearly how racism could cripple white as well as black people."

Wendell Berry echoes this sentiment in his book *The Hidden Wound*. "If the white man has inflicted the wound of racism upon black men, the cost has been that he would receive the mirror image of that wound into himself," he writes. "As master, or a member of the dominant race, he has felt little compulsion to acknowledge it or speak of it; the more painful it has grown the more deeply he has hidden it within himself. But the wound is there, and it is a profound disorder." Berry wants to know this wound more fully—to "cure" it—and to eventually be free of it so he doesn't pass it on.

"The burden of being black and the burden of being white is so heavy that it is rare in our society to experience oneself as a human being," Thurman writes. "It may be, I do not know, that to experience oneself as a human being is one with experiencing one's fellows as human beings. . . . It means that the individual must have a sense of kinship to life that transcends and goes beyond the immediate kinship of family or the organic kinship that binds him ethnically or 'racially' or nationally. . . . To be a human being, then, is to be essentially alive in the world." We must connect with people who look different from ourselves for completion, for healthy wholeness, for true holiness. To possess a liberating spirituality, then, is to reach out and act to restore the kinship, the connection, the oneness. Otherwise, no one is free.

A liberating spirituality frees religion. Thurman struggled to make people aware of how important it is to remove the blockades to community, which is an aspect of God's will. Thurman was particularly frustrated with the exclusivity found among Christian denominations and the exclusivity of Christianity as a whole toward other religions.

For him, much of Christian dogma corrupted the true message of Jesus. Any religion that supports the exploitation of any part of God's beloved creation is inherently misguided. The unwillingness to consider or acknowledge the interconnection of all people fuels much of the injustice in the world. As Katie Cannon so aptly points out, "Fragmented, unfulfilled individuals align their separated lives with all of life, so that as newly empowered individuals, they form community which will allow them to bring insights and concerns of the Christian faith to bear on altering the most oppressive situation in society."

Howard Thurman lived and wrote in a way that was ahead of his time. Although his lectures and sermons attracted people everywhere he went, most church organizations were not ready to consider the significance of the spiritual life or mysticism as a form of religion. These days, however, with spiritual starvation at an all-time high, many people experience a deep yearning for connection and express a greater willingness and openness to his instruction.

How, then, do we pick up the gauntlet he threw down and carry it forward? The answers may be found in accepting our call to sacred activism.

SACRED ACTIVISM

Sacred activists exhibit a reconstructed spirituality. To claim our inner authority and pray for an openness to Inner Authority, we assume our role in the restoration of

God's beloved creation. Many spiritual seekers and most ordinary mystics utilize their inner authority to demand respect for themselves and other human spirits. Sometimes hurdles—personal constraints that reside within our inner lives—prevent us from living from Spirit. The most common hindrances are unhealed wounds, concerns about what others will think, loss of status or financial security, and a refusal to challenge authority. This inner work must be addressed in order to sustain our sacred call.

Howard Thurman set about fulfilling his call to feed the hunger of the human spirit while also tending to the needs of oppressed people all over the world. In turn, he realized that people can, through developing an inner spirituality, summon the strength and vitality to live as sacred activists. Thurman's living wisdom is exactly what is needed to support sacred activism in the world today. He set the spiritual groundwork for the civil rights movement through his constant communion with the living presence of God. Both Thurman and Gandhi believed that without the individual pursuit of the spiritual life, social transformation becomes unattainable.

Once on the spiritual path, how do we discern our unique sacred call? Developing what Thurman called a "working paper" may lead us there. Among the questions Thurman proposed, these flash like a bright neon sign: "What are you trying to do? What does it mean to commit your life? What does life mean to you? Do you have your own working paper or are you using one that you just borrowed from somebody?"

By "working paper," Thurman meant a statement that describes your sense of God's purpose in your life and the daily practices you engage in to live it out. In three unpublished sermons, Thurman offered details of a working paper in three unpublished sermons, Ellison writes. Ellison characterizes a working paper in this way: "a living document that is subject to revision and refinement as dictated by the Spirit of God and the daily life lessons." A working paper brings a certain clarity to our lives; otherwise we act like unleased office space—available for rent to the highest bidder. Our motivations often emerge from the economic or social marketplace rather than from deep searching.

These probing questions remain with us. They moved me to establish my own working paper, and perhaps they will do the same for you. My initial working paper includes these statements: *My early connection to Spirit via the wind held my sacred call until I became conscious of it. My purpose is to companion others as they become aware of the Spirit within. It is to midwife the Spirit in others, to help people pause, center down, listen and follow the Guidance.*

My spiritual practice includes pausing and asking Spirit for the next step, the next task. I also inquire of Spirit about what to say and how to structure retreats and lectures. I lean in for deeper guidance when meeting with a person for spiritual companioning. Strengthening my commitment to God helps to ward off the many diversions—money, celebrity, material accumulations—that fail to benefit anyone other than me and my family.

What might you write in your own working paper? What is your understanding of your sacred call, and how do you live it out daily? How might it be linked to what makes you come alive?

Spirit enlivens all things, and any truly restructured spirituality makes us feel as if we have come alive. It must be formed and sustained by Spirit. An invigorating, awakening spirituality generates a vitality that springs us out of bed and spurs us into action. It helps us listen for the role only we can play in the restoration of God's beloved creation. Spirit nudges us toward the deep peace and jubilant joy of a life centered in God. As we work to restore unity inside and outside of ourselves, we come alive. Like trees, which care for other trees, bear fruit, offer shade, and remind us of our own aliveness, we begin to care for others. Oneness is real. We are utterly dependent on each other. Each morning, as the sun rises over the eastern horizon, our bodies come alive, and our spirituality should do the same. When we've uncovered God's love within us, we allow it to radiate through us and out into the world.

WALKING WITH HOWARD THURMAN

Those fortunate to spend time with Howard Thurman in his last months remarked that he remained a spiritual seeker until the end. As he anticipated his final visit with Howard Thurman in 1981, humanities professor and friend Edward Kaplan expected to encounter a weak man dying from cancer, physical deterioration, and a lifetime battle with asthma. To his surprise and delight, however, Thurman was filled with vitality and talked with Kaplan for more than three hours. They discussed a number of Kaplan's personal issues, and Thurman, with his penetrating yet gentle interrogation, left Kaplan stunned, grateful, and with more questions than when he arrived.

Sue, Thurman's wife, reported that in his final days in bed, as he moved in and out of consciousness, he continued to question the meaning of universal matters. Always an inquisitive soul, Thurman knew there was more to excavate, to discover, to contribute. He told Sue that "he encountered the 'particular' man and the 'universal man' within himself and wrestled them to earth, until he won the consent of both—to Life, to Death, and back to Life." Howard Thurman passed away on April 10, 1981, at the age of eighty-one.

As I complete my walk with Howard Thurman, I feel refreshed, renewed, alive. Thurman has affirmed and normalized my early mystical inclinations. I still feel drawn to the mystical realms of most faith traditions. Inspired by the poetry of Rumi and Hafiz, I find myself reading more widely about Sufism. I want to learn more about the Kabbalah and Jewish approaches to mysticism. I also cherish the Baptist and Buddhist roots of my first meditation teacher, Jan Willis. I understand that within each of these lies a reminder to live in the present moment—in the presence of God. I want to inspire everyone to open their hearts to all the ways that God wants to connect with them. Catching a quiet lull in the busyness or a wisp of stillness outside is the easiest way to rendezvous with my Creator. For others, a visit from the Divine Guest may appear during the Eucharist, a soulfully rendered gospel song, a heartfelt sermon, a rhythmic chant, or a whirling dance.

These days, as I walk past the painting of Howard Thurman, which sits on a carved wooden tripod in the foyer outside my bedroom, I offer a grateful prayer for Bec, who thrust the portrait into my hands years ago in the mountains of North Carolina. He gazes in my direction with a hint of a smile. Thurman left us a treasure trove of wisdom, and I sense he doesn't want it to remain hidden or ignored.

By assuming his sacred call, Howard Thurman planted the seeds for a different spirituality than the one he saw around him. His spirit still calls us to tend to these now grown trees, to live the prayers he prayed, and to move closer to his dream of community. Each of us can imagine a reformed spirituality, but how can we bring it to fruition?

I imagine asking Thurman this question. I think he would smile broadly. I think he would remind us that we have all the spiritual tools we need. He may have delivered the blueprint for a liberating spirituality, but now we must build the structure. As our walk with Thurman ends, we roll up our sleeves and gather the resources he left. We get to work on living a liberating, active, and mystical spirituality that makes us come alive.

REFLECTION QUESTIONS

- What does reading about Howard Thurman stir in you?
- How can you reconstruct your spiritual life so that it liberates you and others?

- What hindrances do you foresee if you choose to live as an everyday mystic?

- What prevents you from feeling a sense of community, of oneness?

SPIRITUAL STEPS

- Compassionately observe how you respond to human spirits who appear different from you. What gets triggered—fear, anger, competition, threat? Which of your own unacknowledged attributes might you project on them? Continue this spiritual practice until mercy and love begin to fill your heart.

- Compose your "working paper." Revise it periodically to meet changing life demands and the promptings of Spirit.

- What unhealed wounds may keep you from examining your inner life and adjusting your spiritual life?

- Go do something that makes you come alive.

- Be intentional about doing three or more things that are loving this week. Maybe one or two of the acts are for yourself because you are the one most in need of the love. Be intentional about being loving, kind, and caring, especially toward strangers.

ACKNOWLEDGMENTS

I am grateful and deeply indebted to so many people who walked with me toward the completion of this book. First and foremost to Bec Cranford, for the portrait of Howard Thurman that planted the seeds in my mind for a book about him for spiritual seekers.

I wish to thank you, Luther Smith Jr., for your seminal book on Howard Thurman, our table fellowships, and your treasured wisdom, and I extend special thanks to Walter Earl Fluker, Peter Eisenstadt, Kai Jackson, and others for creating a treasury of previously inaccessible material on Howard Thurman. In particular, *The Papers of Howard Washington Thurman*, *Volumes 1–5* and your authored books on Howard Thurman proved invaluable to my writing.

I offer my heartfelt appreciation to J. Bernard Kynes and Jan Willis for encouraging me to tarry with Howard Thurman because there is always more to learn, to know, and to explore.

I am especially indebted to Carl McColman for his gentle nudging and recommendation to lead my first Howard Thurman retreats. On several occasions Carl, Cassidy Hall, Kevin Johnson, Lisa Cólon DeLay, Tom Bushlack, and Debonee Morgan invited me to join them on their podcasts to talk about Howard Thurman—thank you. Similarly, I extend my warmest gratitude to Margaret Benefiel and the staff at the Shalem Institute for the invitation to create two online retreats on Howard Thurman, which allow him to continue to feed the hunger of the human spirit.

Without my precious readers and contributors— Isa Williams, Phillip Johnson, Joan Murray, Stuart Higginbotham, Sabbaye McGriff, and Terresa Ford—this book would lack flavor and texture. Thank you for enriching it.

To my spiritual advisers and friends who held my vision and supported me with love, faith, and prayers—Fay Key, Lea Robinson, Steve Bullington, Oliver Ferrari, Jocelyn Lyons, Marquita Bradley, Shay Dowley, Florida Ellis, Linda Bryant, Betty Cunningham, Maggie Winfrey, and Rebecca Parker—I thank you for your vigilance and sage counsel whenever I seemed unsure of my way.

I also wish to acknowledge Fay Acker, Aljosie Aldrich Harding, Peggy Thompson, Juarlyn Gaiter, Corey Brown, Therese Taylor-Stinson, Brenda Bertrand, and JoAnn Stewart Moore for connecting me to several people and resources.

I appreciate the prayers and relentless support of Clarence Coleman, Lisa Wells, Tracy Walker, Mette Riis, Camille Brown, Columbus Brown II, Leah Nichelle Brown, Carson Brown, Natasha Browder, Debra Mixon Mitchell, and numerous spiritual companions who continue to sustain me with many forms of spiritual and emotional care.

Without the discerning and extremely knowledgeable eyes of my wise, gentle, and marvelous editor, Valerie

Weaver-Zercher, my words would not begin to capture the beauty and depth of Howard Thurman's wisdom. Thank you for seeing what remained hidden to me.

What a sacred synchronicity and clear gift from Spirit you are, Ed DeVan. As my former student who parachuted back into my life, your extraordinary research and editorial skills and indomitable spirit remain priceless. I will forever be thankful for your enormous contribution to this project.

I have no words to express my gratitude for my loving and caring husband, Columbus Brown, who shares my deep appreciation for Howard Thurman, for making time for several Howard Thurman retreats, cooking many meals, and listening patiently. I cherish our love and partnership.

I wish I could personally thank Howard Thurman for his sheer devotion and dedication to God and his call. The hours and energy he willingly gave in service to his mission to move us closer to community, our common unity, are exemplary.

Most of all, I wish to acknowledge Sophia, my nickname for Spirit, which lies within my being and continues to supply me with strength, unfathomable wisdom, and daily guidance to face whatever appears on my spiritual path.

RECOMMENDED READING LIST

Author Note: This is not an exhaustive list of Thurman's publications but includes the ones that most connect to each chapter, along with several books about Thurman.

CHAPTER 1

Howard Thurman, *With Head and Heart: The Autobiography of Howard Thurman* (New York: NY, Harcourt & Brace, 1979).

Howard Thurman, *Meditations of the Heart* (Boston: Beacon Press, 1981).

Howard Thurman, *Deep Is the Hunger: Meditations for Apostles of Sensitiveness* (Richmond, IN: Friends United Press, 2000).

CHAPTER 2

Howard Thurman, *Meditations of the Heart* (Boston: Beacon Press, 1981).

Howard Thurman, *Disciplines of the Spirit* (Richmond, Indiana: Friends United Press, 1963).

CHAPTER 3

Howard Thurman, *The Growing Edge* (Richmond, IN: Friends United Press, 1998).

Alton B. Pollard III, *Mysticism and Social Change: The Social Witness of Howard Thurman* (New York: Peter Lang, 1992).

CHAPTER 4

Howard Thurman, *Jesus and the Disinherited* (Boston: Beacon Press, 1976).

Luther Smith Jr., *Howard Thurman: The Mystic as Prophet* (Richmond, IN: Friends United Press, 1991).

CHAPTER 5

Howard Thurman, *Footprints of a Dream: The Story of the Church for the Fellowship of All Peoples* (Eugene, OR: Wipe and Stock Publishers, 1959).

Quinton Dixie and Peter Eisenstadt, *Visions of a Better World: Howard Thurman's Pilgrimage to India and the Origins of African American Nonviolence* (Boston, MA: Beacon Press, 2011).

Peter Eisenstadt, *Against the Hounds of Hell: A Life of Howard Thurman* (Charlottesville: University of Virginia Press, 2021).

CHAPTER 6

Howard Thurman, *Jesus and the Disinherited* (Boston: Beacon Press, 1976).

Howard Thurman, *The Mood of Christmas & Other Celebrations* (Richmond, IN: Friends United Press, 2011).

Anthony C. Siracusa, *Nonviolence Before King: The Politics of Being and the Black Freedom Struggle* (Chapel Hill: University of North Carolina Press, 2021).

CHAPTER 7

Howard Thurman, *Mysticism and the Experience of Love* (Wallingford, PA: Pendle Hill Publications, 2015).

Howard Thurman, *The Creative Encounter: An Interpretation of Religion and the Social Witness* (Richmond, IN: Friends United Press, 1972).

Peter Eisenstadt and Walter Earl Fluker, eds., *The Way of the Mystics: Howard Thurman* (Maryknoll, NY: Orbis Books, 2021).

CHAPTER 8

Howard Thurman, *The Inward Journey* (Richmond, IN: Friends United Press, 2007).

Howard Thurman, *Deep Is the Hunger* (Richmond, IN: Friends United Press, 2000).

Luther Smith Jr., *Howard Thurman: The Mystic as Prophet* (Richmond, IN: Friends United Press, 1991).

CHAPTER 9

Gregory C. Ellison III, ed., *Anchored in the Current: Discovering Howard Thurman as Educator, Activist, Guide, and Prophet* (Louisville, KY: Westminster John Knox, 2020).

George K. Makechnie, *Howard Thurman: His Enduring Dream* (Boston: The Howard Thurman Center, Boston University, 1988).

The Living Wisdom of Howard Thurman: A Visionary for Our Time, audio recording (Boulder, CO: Sounds True, 2010).

CHAPTER 10

Howard Thurman, *The Luminous Darkness: A Personal Interpretation of the Anatomy of Segregation and the Ground of Hope* (Richmond, IN: Friends United Press,1989).

Howard Thurman, *The Search for Common Ground: An Inquiry into the Basis of Man's Experience of Community* (Richmond, IN: Friends United Press, 1986).

Howard Thurman, *The Centering Moment* (Richmond, IN: Friends United Press, 2007).

NOTES

CHAPTER 1

as Marsha Sinetar refers to them Marsha Sinetar, *Ordinary People as Monks and Mystics: Lifestyles for Spiritual Wholeness* (New York: Paulist Press, 2007).

"living with a sensitivity . . . hiding like Zacchaeus." Albert Haase, *Becoming an Ordinary Mystic: Spirituality for the Rest of Us* (Downers Grove, IL: InterVarsity Press, 2019), 3.

"Don't ask . . . people who have come alive." Gil Bailie, *Violence Unveiled: Humanity at the Crossroads* (New York: Crossroads Publishing, 1995), xv.

"He began to sketch . . . the 'very Jesus contribution' he envisioned." Anthony C. Siracusa, *Nonviolence Before King: The Politics of Being and the Black Freedom Struggle* (Chapel Hill: University of North Carolina Press, 2021), 62.

"He had a great zest . . . the task of spiritual reconstruction." Paul Harvey, *Howard Thurman and the Disinherited: A Religious Biography* (Grand Rapids: Eerdmans Press, 2020) 221.

CHAPTER 2

"How good is it to center" Thurman, *Meditations of the Heart*, (Boston: Beacon Press, 1981), 15.

three pillars of the spiritual path Anne D. LeClaire, *Listening Below the Noise: The Transformative Power of Silence* (New York: Harper Perennial, 2009), 35.

NOTES

I was a very sensitive child . . . my ambition to get an education. Howard Thurman, *Footprints of a Dream: The Story of the Church for the Fellowship of All Peoples* (Eugene, OR: Wipf & Stock, 2009), 16.

"When I was young . . . the aliveness of the woods." Howard Thurman, *With Head and Heart: The Autobiography of Howard Thurman* (New York: Harcourt Brace & Company, 1979), 7.

"Thus began one of my most memorable friendships . . . interspersed by other vocal prayers." Kenneth Cober, *Tales out of School* (New York: Cortland, 1995), 22.

and in the quiet For example, see Mark 1:35, Luke 5:15–16, Luke 6:12–13, Mark 1:45, Mark 3:13, Mark 6:31–32, Mark 6:46, Mathew 14:13, and Matthew 14:23.

"This was the time . . . the heart and mind." Howard Thurman, *The Inward Journey* (Richmond, IN: Friends United Press, 2007), 30.

We must find . . . cessation from churning. Howard Thurman, *Deep Is the Hunger* (Richmond, IN: Friends United Press, 2000), 175–76.

later excerpted in **Visions of a Better World: Howard Thurman's Pilgrimage to India** Quinton Dixie and Peter Eisenstadt, *Visions of a Better World: Howard Thurman's Pilgrimage to India and the Origins of African American Nonviolence* (Boston: Beacon Press, 2011).

Nobody said a word . . . in the presence of God. Howard Thurman, "Meaning of Commitment #5: Strength of Corporate Worship," April 8, 1951, http://hgar-srv3.bu.edu/web/howard-thurman/virtual-listening-room/detail?id=341417.

"When the American learns . . . to face the world." Elizabeth Yates, *Howard Thurman: Portrait of a Practical Dreamer* (New York: The John Day Company, 1964), 99.

future thinking about silence Luther Smith Jr., *Howard Thurman: The Mystic as Prophet* (Richmond, IN: Friends United Press, 1991).

"allow the inspiration of the words to hold full sway." Thurman, *With Head and Heart*, 93.

In my opinion the most important part . . . rare and holy celebration. Thurman, *Footprints of a Dream*, 70.

back of the weekly bulletin Thurman, *Meditations of the Heart*, 13.

"This quiet period . . . to seek any other help." Thurman, *Footprints of a Dream*, 71.

"meet her in the silence . . . separating us at all." Thurman, *With Head and Heart*, 159.

"Prayer is not only the participation . . . the spirit for the experience." Howard Thurman, *The Creative Encounter: An Interpretation of Religion and the Social Witness* (Richmond, IN: Friends United Press, 1972), 34.

"There is silence . . . his particular needs." Howard Thurman, *Disciplines of the Spirit* (Richmond, IN: Friends United Press, 1963), 97.

"Thurman specifically described . . . Thurman drew strength every day." Rev. Wayne B. Arnason, "What's Love Got to Do With it: The Mysticism of Howard Thurman" (paper prepared for Prairie Group, November 2010, accessed July 30, 2017, http://prairiegroupuu.org/images/2010.Thurman.Arnason.paper.pdf), 8.

"our minds seethe . . . or a 'remembered radiance.'" Thurman, *Disciplines of the Spirit*, 98.

a form of torture Anne D. LeClaire, *Listening Below the Noise*, 83.

"Those who have been traumatized . . . back to consciousness." Barbara Holmes, *Joy Unspeakable: Contemplative Practices of the Black Church*, 2nd ed. (Minneapolis: Fortress Press, 2017), 7.

feel too unsettling Holmes, *Joy Unspeakable*.

"the love of God" for healing This suggestion is mentioned in *The Creative Encounter* and also in the meditation "I Yield to Thee" in *Meditations of the Heart*.

"As frightening as it may be . . . first steps toward restoration." Holmes, *Joy Unspeakable*, 22.

Once the interference . . . the freedom it inspires. Thurman, *Disciplines of the Spirit*, 99–100.

CHAPTER 3

"The ocean and the night . . . in nature, in existence." Thurman, *With Head and Heart*, 8.

As a child . . . There was God. Thurman, *Disciplines of the Spirit*, 96.

NOTES

"the harmony of creation." Howard Thurman, *The Search for Common Ground: An Inquiry into the Basis of Man's Experience of Community* (Richmond, IN: Friends United Press, 1986), 18.

"The signature of God . . . the minds of men." Thurman, *Deep Is the Hunger*, 212.

"A candidate's acceptance . . . the religious community." Margaret Washington Creel, *"A Peculiar People": Slave Religion and Community-Culture Among the Gullah*s (New York: New York University Press, 1981), 285.

"While 'seekin' culminated . . . 'thing' by the master." Creel, *"A Peculiar People"*, 295.

"I needed the strength . . . know that it understood." Thurman, *With Head and Heart*, 9.

inner reserves of the Creator Thurman, *Deep is the Hunger*, 170.

damaging to them Peter Wohlleben, *The Hidden Life of Trees: How They Feel, How They Communicate—Discoveries from a Secret World* (Vancouver, BC: Greystone Books), 2016.

keep them alive Susan Simard, *Finding the Mother Tree: Discovering the Wisdom of the Forest* (New York: Alfred A. Knopf, 2021), 289.

forest fire forces it out Thurman, *Meditations of the Heart*, 82.

There is inherent . . . inherent in the tree. Howard Thurman, *The Growing Edge* (Richmond, IN: Friends United Press, 1998), 177.

We are most alive . . . prayer at its best and highest. Thurman, *The Inward Journey*, 19–20.

"I cannot escape . . . infinite series of yesterdays." Howard Thurman, *Deep River: An Interpretation of Negro Spirituals* (Oakland, CA: The Eucalyptus Press, 1945), 35.

"It is the flood . . . flood time of the river." Thurman, *Deep River*, 37.

"The goal and the source . . . The source of life is God!" Thurman, *Deep River*, 38.

"It [a dream] must be . . . in the light of the sun." George Makechnie, *Howard Thurman: His Enduring Dream* (Boston: The Howard Thurman Center, Boston University, 1988), 9.

"We are utterly dependent . . . dependence is evident everywhere." Thurman, *The Growing Edge*, 150–51.

Near the end of our journey . . . behavior patterns of those involved. Thurman, *Footprints of a Dream*, 24.

"He remembered the day . . . a storm was coming." Yates, *Portrait of a Practical Dreamer*, 29.

"less than a year old . . . at a conscious level." Thurman, *The Search for Common Ground*, 57–58.

"Nature was an enemy . . . too busy to listen." Yates, *Portrait of a Practical Dreamer*, 98–99.

Man is a child of nature . . . rape it with impunity. Thurman, *The Search for Common Ground*, 83.

CHAPTER 4

"It was not until my experience . . . much, much more." Thurman, *With Head and Heart*, 15–16. Howard Thurman used the word *self-estimate* for what we now commonly refer to as self-esteem.

"The majestic power . . . and not to yield." Howard Thurman, *Jesus and the Disinherited* (Boston: Beacon Press, 1976), 47.

radical trust in God Marcus J. Borg, *Jesus, A New Vision: Spirit, Culture, and the Life of Discipleship* (San Francisco: HarperSanFrancisco, 1987), 111.

"It goes back to my childhood . . . external judgment of me [as a Black man]." Mozella G. Mitchell, "Religion and the Discovery of Self: Howard Thurman and the Tributaries of the Deep River," in *The Religion Factor: An Introduction to How Religion Matters*, eds. William S. Green and Jacob Neusner (Louisville, KY: Westminster John Knox Press, 1996), 94.

sisters' spirits felt revived Thurman, *With Head and Heart*, 20–21.

"Nancy Ambrose was the first . . . definition to one's being." Smith, *Howard Thurman*, 40–41.

"I have seen it happen . . . has even been transcended." Thurman, *Jesus and the Disinherited*, 45.

God loves them too Many years after Howard Thurman's apt discernment about the spiritual nature of the self, research has documented the assertion that humans are neurologically pre-wired for spirituality. Contemporary research confirms the protective factors associated with the combination of spirituality and parenting, also referred to as the "intergenerational transmission of spirituality." This psycho-familial-spiritual and universal phenomenon is characterized by a loving parent, grandparent, or engaged adult communicating a sense of transcendent love (God's love). The method may include prayer, spiritual practices, church attendance, or continual shared awareness of spiritual presence. The child observes the spirituality of the parent or spiritual figure and follows their example while also feeling deeply cared for by them. Seen in a variety of faith traditions (e.g., Hinduism, Islam, Judaism), the intergenerational transmission of spirituality maintains a preventive element against alcohol use, depression, and risk-taking in children and adolescents. For more, see Lisa Miller and Theresa Barker, *The Spiritual Child: The New Science on Parenting for Health and Lifelong Thriving* (New York: St. Martin's Press, 2015), 88.

"The doom of the children . . . for them is abnormal." Thurman, *Jesus and the Disinherited*, 44.

with a true sense of self Smith, *Howard Thurman*, 54.

In order to answer the questions . . . a sense of self. Thurman, *Deep is the Hunger*, 63.

"The psychological effect . . . whatever he does." Thurman, *Jesus and the Disinherited*, 43.

"many divisions within . . . speaks within us." Thurman, *The Inward Journey*, 135.

Thurman pictures various voices . . . is similarly achieved. Mozella G. Mitchell, "Religion and the Discovery of Self: Howard Thurman and the Tributaries of the Deep River," in *The Religion Factor: An Introduction to How Religion Matters*, eds. William S. Green and Jacob Neusner (Louisville, KY: Westminster John Knox Press, 1996), 159–60.

"The awareness of being a child . . . again and again." Thurman, *Jesus and the Disinherited*, 39.

"Often there are things . . . trembling as to God." Howard Thurman, "Good News for the Underprivileged," in *The Papers of Howard*

Washington Thurman, ed. Walter Earl Fluker, vol. 1, *My People Need Me, June 1918–March 1936* (Columbia, SC: University of South Carolina Press, 2009), 265.

"Stripped to the literal substance . . . in our own sight?" Thurman, *Deep Is the Hunger,* 62.

"'Oneness' is an easy enough thing . . . it's everybody." Liza J. Rankow, "Mysticism and Social Action: The Ethical Demands of Oneness," in *Anchored in the Current: Discovering Howard Thurman as Educator, Activist, Guide, and Prophet,* ed. Gregory C. Ellison II (Louisville, KY: Westminster John Knox, 2020), 119.

"Jesus demonstrated . . . classification of enemy." Thurman, *Jesus and the Disinherited,* 87.

"There is something . . . somebody else pulls." Howard Thurman, "The Sound of the Genuine," *The Spelman Messenger* 96, no. 4 (Summer 1980): 14–15.

CHAPTER 5

the eighth-grade exam Thurman, *With Head and Heart,* 23.

"word in my heart." Thurman, *With Head and Heart,* 169.

"Providence would be . . . a railway station." Peter Eisenstadt, *Against the Hounds of Hell: A Life of Howard Thurman* (Charlottesville, VA: University of Virginia Press, 2021), 46.

remainder of high school Howard Thurman, *With Head and Heart,* 25–26.

continue his education Landrum Bolling, "Conversations with Howard Thurman, Part 1," YouTube video, 58 minutes, August 27, 2015.

"When I was born . . . there was no escape." Jean Burden, "Meditation on Howard Thurman on the Occasion of His Memorial Service April 10, 1981," Howard Thurman Papers Project File, Boston University.

calling him to for years Howard Thurman, *Footprints of a Dream,* 18.

"that which moves with the grain in my own wood." Howard Thurman, "Mysticism and Social Change: Rufus Jones," in *The Way of the Mystics: Howard Thurman,* eds. Peter Eisenstadt and Walter Earl Fluker (Maryknoll, NY: Orbis Books, 2021), 141.

According to his autobiography . . . pregnant with deeper significance. Dixie and Eisenstadt, *Visions of a Better World*, 98–99.

three hours for their exchange Dixie and Eisenstadt, *Visions of a Better World*, 99.

a force superior to brutality Dixie and Eisenstadt, *Visions of a Better World*, 105.

"The cosmos is the kind . . . of harmony and integration." Dixie and Eisenstadt, *Visions of a Better World*, 105.

Martin Luther King Jr. was born *The Papers of Howard Washington Thurman*, ed. Walter Earl Fluker, vol. 4, *The Soundless Passion of a Single Mind, June 1949–December 1962* (Columbia, SC: University of South Carolina Press, 2017), xxvi.

crossed paths in significant ways Eisenstadt, *Against the Hounds of Hell*, 284.

together and talking *The Papers of Howard Washington Thurman*, vol. 4, xxvi.

congregation's opening celebration Thurman, *Footprints of a Dream*, 40–41.

CHAPTER 6

for a real Christian Howard Thurman, "Jesus and the Disinherited #1," 1959, http://hgar-srv3.bu.edu/web/howard-thurman/virtual-listening-room/detail?id=370839.

he was seeing it practiced Thurman, "Jesus and the Disinherited #1," http://hgar-srv3.bu.edu/web/howard-thurman/virtual-listening-room/detail?id=370839.

"Why Paul could feel . . . appeal to Caesar." Howard Thurman, "Good News for the Underprivileged," 263–269.

deserving of worship Howard Thurman, "The Significance of Jesus II: The Temptation of Jesus," in *The Papers of Howard Washington Thurman*, ed. Walter Earl Fluker, vol. 2, *Who Calls Me Christian?, April 1936–August 1943* (Columbia, SC: University of South Carolina Press, 2012), 54–60.

If we accept . . . the very heart of God. Thurman, "The Significance of Jesus II," 62.

NOTES

"It seems in this prayer . . . presence of God." Howard Thurman, "The Significance of Jesus IV: Prayer Life of Jesus," in *The Papers of Howard Washington Thurman*, ed. Walter Earl Fluker, vol. 2, *Who Calls Me Christian?, April 1936–August 1943* (Columbia, SC: University of South Carolina Press, 2012), 70.

"to him God . . . my deepest needs." Thurman, "The Significance of Jesus IV," 73.

"What is most expedient?" Howard Thurman, "Jesus and the Disinherited #3," 1959, http://hgar-srv3.bu.edu/web/howard-thurman/vuisirtual-listening-room/detail?id=371328.

a prominent role Bart D. Erhman, *The Triumph of Christianity: How a Forbidden Religion Swept the World* (New York: Simon & Schuster, 2019), 283.

"What do you do . . . situation of oppression?" Howard Thurman, "Jesus and the Disinherited #2," http://hgar-srv3.bu.edu/web/howard-thurman/virtual-listening-room/detail?id=3713251959.

"people who stand with their backs against the wall" Thurman, *Jesus and the Disinherited*, xix.

kingdom of God is at hand Mark 1:15.

stable sense of self Smith, *Howard Thurman*, 108–9.

"He recognized with authentic realism . . . exercise power over him." Thurman, *Jesus and the Disinherited*, 18.

"The prophetic nature . . . little old me!" Thurman, *Jesus and the Disinherited*, 45.

"If a man continues . . . toward each other." Thurman, *Jesus and the Disinherited*, 54, 59.

affirmed Thurman's convictions Dixie and Eisenstadt, *Visions of a Better World*, 107–8.

"Unwavering sincerity says . . . nothing is hidden." Thurman, *Jesus and the Disinherited*, 61.

"To love such people . . . the human spirit." Thurman, *Jesus and the Disinherited*, 84.

"freed spirits." Thurman, *Jesus and the Disinherited*, 91.

"Strong enough means . . . loves one's enemies," Mitzi J. Smith, "Howard Thurman and the Religion of Jesus: Survival of the Disinherited and Womanist Wisdom," *Journal for the Study of the Historical Jesus* 17 (2019): 280.

"Instead of relation . . . moment of human dignity." Thurman, *Jesus and the Disinherited*, 63.

"When we love . . . tall enough to wear it." Howard Thurman, "Good News for the Underprivileged," 269.

filled with bedbugs Pauli Murray, *Song in a Weary Throat: Memoir of an American Pilgrimage* (New York: Liveright Publishing, 2018), 185.

"She recalled that . . . deeply rooted and sincere." Anthony Siracusa, *Nonviolence Before King*, 85.

CHAPTER 7

"center down." See his lovely and popular meditation "How Good to Center Down," in *Meditations of the Heart*, 28–29.

"In the total religious experience . . . to Himself in me." Luther E. Smith Jr., *Howard Thurman: Essential Writings* (Maryknoll, NY: Orbis Books, 2006), 45.

"God bottoms existence." Eisenstadt and Fluker, *Way of the Mystics*, 127.

Every day after breakfast . . . a sense of Presence. Kerry Walters, ed., *Rufus Jones: Essential Writings* (Maryknoll, NY: Orbis Books), 40.

"distinction between cloistered . . . and its concerns." Dixie and Eisenstadt, *Visions of a Better World*, 50.

mysticism for the masses Peter Eisenstadt and Walter Earl Fluker, eds., *Way of the Mystics* (Maryknoll, NY: Orbis Books), 149.

"He contended that . . . and the world," Alton B. Pollard III, *Mysticism and Social Change: The Social Witness of Howard Thurman* (New York: Peter Lang, 1992), 33.

gift to Howard Thurman Pollard III, *Mysticism and Social Change*, 34.

"So, I tolerated . . . in my thinking." Peter Eisenstadt and Walter Earl Fluker, eds., *Way of the Mystics* (Maryknoll, NY: Orbis Books), 158.

NOTES

"the response of the individual . . . within his own spirit." Howard Thurman, *Mysticism and the Experience of Love—Pendle Hill Pamphlet 115* (Wallingford, PA: Pendle Hill Publications, 1961), 6.

numerology or psychic endeavors Thurman, *Mysticism and the Experience of Love*, 66.

"Mysticism and Social Change." *The Papers of Howard Washington Thurman*, ed. Walter Earl Fluker, vol. 2, *Who Calls Me Christian?, April 1936–August 1943* (Columbia, SC: University of South Carolina Press, 2012), 190–222.

"He knows that he cannot escape . . . his actions valid." *The Papers of Howard Washington Thurman*, vol. 2, 217.

"the nerve center of his consent . . . he lives or dies." Thurman, *Disciplines of the Spirit*, 17.

"overall approach to mysticism . . . of the population." Pollard, *Mysticism and Social Change*, 27.

The central fact . . . of profound importance. Thurman, *The Creative Encounter*, 23–24.

"rediscovery of the eternal" that was always present Charles Bennett, *A Philosophical Study of Mysticism.* Cited in Thurman, *Mysticism and the Experience of Love*, Location 107.

"The central question . . . and reconditioning process." Thurman, *The Creative Encounter*, 85–86.

"Despite the personal character . . . companions along the way." Thurman, *Disciplines of the Spirit*, 77.

"concern for inward journeys . . . turns them outward again." Douglas V. Steere, "Don't Forget Those Leather Gloves," in *Common Ground: Essays in Honor of Howard Thurman on the Occasion of his Seventy-Fifth Birthday, November 18, 1975*, ed. Samuel Lucius Gandy (Washington, DC: Hoffman Press, 1976), iii.

"You can only spend . . . earned in contemplation." Steere, "Don't Forget Those Leather Gloves," iii.

"Mystical consciousness . . . for a ministry of love." Howard Thurman, "Mysticism and Jesus" (Lecture V, University of Redlands, May 1973),

quoted in Luther Smith Jr., *Howard Thurman: The Mystic as Prophet* (Richmond, IN: Friends United Press, 1991), 65.

"participated at the level . . . after they march." This was cited in Alton Pollard, *Mysticism and Social Change*, 113 and articulated by him in the documentary film *Backs Against the Wall: The Howard Thurman Story*, directed by Martin Doblmeier (Alexandria, VA: Journey Films, 2019), DVD, 57 min.

"is an expression of resistance . . . this calls for action." Howard Thurman, "Mysticism and Social Action" (Lawrence Lecture on Religion and Society, First Unitarian Church of Berkeley, October 13, 1978), quoted in Alton Pollard, *Mysticism and Social Change*, 65.

CHAPTER 8

There is in every person . . . of your inner authority. Thurman, *Meditations of the Heart*, 15.

"A new self emerges . . . more and more organized." Howard Thurman, "The Religion of the Inner Life" (sermon delivered to Fellowship Church, San Francisco, CA, 1950), reprinted in Eisenstadt and Fluker, eds., *The Way of the Mystics*, 117–118.

in all human beings See Kevin Quashie, *The Sovereignty of Quiet: Beyond Resistance in Black Culture* (New Brunswick, NJ: Rutgers University Press, 2012) for an expanded exposition of this premise.

"But whether the acceptance . . . sense of values to be so." Howard Thurman, *The Luminous Darkness: A Personal Interpretation of the Anatomy of Segregation and the Ground of Hope* (Richmond, IN: Friends United Press,1989), 65.

"This island is a bastion . . . breached without consent." Holmes, *Joy Unspeakable*, 4.

"Each person's life . . . each mystical experience." Katie G. Cannon, *Black Womanist Ethics* (Eugene, OR: Wipe and Stock, 1988), 21.

"She acted as one . . . exercised control over it." Smith, *Howard Thurman*, 173.

NOTES

shaped his destiny The Papers of Howard Washington Thurman, ed. Walter Earl Fluker, vol. 3, *The Bold Adventure, September 1943–May 1949* (Columbia, SC: University of South Carolina Press, 2015), 25.

"It was my discovery . . . on his street," Howard Thurman, "Mysticism and Social Change" (lecture, Pacific School of Religion, Berkeley, CA, July 19, 1978), quoted in Alton Pollard, *Mysticism and Social Change,* 112.

"I didn't have to wait . . . it was in me." Mary E. Goodwin, "Racial Roots and Religion: An Interview with Howard Thurman," *The Christian Century* 90 (May 9, 1973): 533–35, quoted in Walter Earl Fluker and Catherine Tumber, eds., *A Strange Freedom: The Best of Howard Thurman on Religious Experience and Public Life* (Boston, MA: Beacon Press, 1998), 12.

baring his soul Smith, *Howard Thurman,* 190.

fruit of the Spirit Lisa Colón DeLay, *The Wild Land Within: Cultivating Wholeness Through Spiritual Practice* (Minneapolis: Broadleaf Books, 2021), 177.

"The quality of the inner life . . . the spiritual life." Smith, *Howard Thurman,* 64.

"The inner life . . . offspring of God." Howard Thurman, "The Inner Life and World-Mindedness," in Justin Wroe Nixon and Winthrop Still Hudson, eds., *Christian Leadership in World Society: Essays in Honor of CONRAD HENRY MOEHLMAN* (Rochester, NY: The Colgate-Rochester Divinity School, 1945), 188.

"places at the center . . . beauty, and fullness." Thurman, "The Inner Life and World-Mindedness," 190.

"My inner world . . . terrains for a lifetime." DeLay, *The Wild Land Within,* 1–2.

"By relying on Absolute Authority . . . inherently in each person." Reunion, "Absolute Authority & Inner Authority with Fr. Richard Rohr," YouTube video, 7:05, May 23, 2018, https://www.youtube.com › watch?v=-AuJYD3wyIE.

"Thurman was inspired . . . for wisdom and faith," Smith, *Howard Thurman,* 187.

"It takes strength . . . He has come into His own." Thurman, *Meditations of the Heart,* 53.

"The eye of the heart . . . even from ourselves." Rose Mary Dougherty, *Discernment: A Path to Spiritual Awakening* (New York: Paulist Press, 2009), 20.

know our true selves Thomas Kelly, *A Testament to Devotion* (New York: Harper & Row, 1941), 117.

waiting for Inner Authority Thurman, *With Head and Heart*, 169.

"there seemed to sound . . . become your friends.'" Zarena Lee, *The Life and Religious Experience of Jarena Lee, A Coloured Lady, Giving Account of her Call to Preach the Gospel*, in William L. Andrews, ed., *Sisters of the Spirit: Three Black Women's Autobiographies of the Nineteenth Century* (Bloomington: Indiana University Press, 1986), 35.

"There must be a change . . . a proper sense of self." Smith, *Howard Thurman*, 199.

CHAPTER 9

"vividly, intensely, personally" Makechnie, *Howard Thurman*, 51.

"For Thurman, real learning . . . so important to him." Dixie and Eisenstadt, *Visions of a Better World*, 50–51.

"Grandmother Nancy . . . shaping, and development." Makechnie, *Howard Thurman*, 11.

"I want to be a minister . . . and follow Him," The Papers of Howard Washington Thurman, vol. 1, xlvii.

"Keep in close touch . . . you can give." Harvey, *Howard Thurman and the Disinherited*, 19.

"had a greater influence . . . into his presence." The Papers of Howard Washington Thurman, vol. 1, lix.

plight of Negroes The Papers of Howard Washington Thurman, vol. 1, lxix

"the huge share . . . with you at Haverford." The Papers of Howard Washington Thurman, vol. 1, 152.

As a result of a series . . . was Martin Luther King Jr. Thurman, *The Search for Common Ground*, 95.

"Thurman was a private man . . . meditation, and prayer." Harvey, *Howard Thurman and the Disinherited*, 7.

"a spiritual uplift . . . that trying period." The Papers of Howard Washington Thurman, vol. 4, 232.

Alice Walker and Barack Obama Vincent Harding, "Introduction," *The Living Wisdom of Howard Thurman: A Visionary for Our Time*, audio recording (Boulder, CO: Sounds True, 2010).

"Still, as in the days . . . precious in God's sight." Marian Wright Edelman, "Prophetic Service and Global Change," in *Anchored in the Current: Discovering Howard Thurman as Educator, Activist, Guide, and Prophet*, ed. Gregory C. Ellison III (Louisville, KY: Westminster John Knox, 2020), 93.

her minister father's study Marian Wright Edelman, *The Measure of our Success: A Letter to my Children and Yours* (New York: HarperPerennial, 1993), 61.

he visited Spelman Chapel Marian Wright Edelman, *Lanterns: A Memoir of Mentors* (New York, NY: HarperCollins, 2000), 26.

"breath of renewal . . . we are not centered." Edelman, "Prophetic Service and Global Change," 102.

"Thurman offered clarification, hope, and encouragement." Harding, "Introduction."

"I remember going to him . . . I have ever known." Vincent Harding, introduction to *For the Inward Journey: The Writings of Howard Thurman*, by Howard Thurman, comp. by Anne Spencer Thurman (Richmond, IN: Friends United Press, 1984), xiv.

"Follow the grain in your own wood." Sam Keen, *To Love and Be Loved* (New York: Bantam Books, 1999), 230.

"Throughout his career . . . their own questions." Eisenstadt, *Against the Hounds of Hell*, 145.

CHAPTER 10

their own spiritual natures Mozella G. Mitchell, *Spiritual Dynamics of Howard Thurman's Theology* (Bristol, IN: Wyndham Hall Press, 1985), 88.

"The mystical experiences . . . within their world." Joy R. Bostic, *African American Female Mysticism: Nineteenth-Century Religious Activism* (New York, NY: Palgrave Macmillan, 2013).

NOTES

"Our dreams will not rest . . . all of us." Harding, "Introduction."

"The spirituality of Howard Thurman . . . of his nation," Vincent Harding, "Dangerous Spirituality" (address, Rankin Chapel, Howard University, March 10, 1998), https://onbeing.org/blog/dangerous-spirituality/

"Seeing the relationship . . . in spite of my fears." Murray, *Song in a Weary Throat*, 138.

"I suspected that . . . in spite of barriers," Murray, *Song in a Weary Throat*, 137.

"If the white man . . . a profound disorder." Wendell Berry, *The Hidden Wound* (San Francisco: Northpoint Press, 1989), 4.

"The burden of being black . . . alive in the world." Thurman, *The Luminous Darkness*, 94.

"Fragmented, unfulfilled individuals . . . situation in society." Cannon, *Black Womanist Ethics*, 21.

openness to his instruction Fortunately, through his foresight and that of others, recordings of Howard Thurman's sermons and lectures are available online through the virtual listening room at Boston University's Howard Thurman and Sue Bailey Thurman Collection and the Pitt Library, Emory University Candler School of Theology.

social transformation becomes unattainable Dixie and Eisenstadt, *Visions of a Better World*, 108.

"What are you trying . . . borrowed from somebody?" Howard Thurman, "Your Life's Working Paper—Introduction" (unpublished sermon, Marsh Chapel, Boston University, September 26, 1954), quoted in Gregory C. Ellison II, "My Working Paper: Beyond the Mule's Path," *Pastoral Psychology* 69, no. 4 (August 2020): 355, https://doi.org/s11089-020-00921-6. Special note—Howard Thurman's "Your Life's Working Paper—Commitment" is available as an audio recording at http://archives.bu.edu/web/howard-thurman/virtual-listening-room/detail?id=373808.

"a living document . . . daily life lessons." Gregory C. Ellison II, "My Working Paper: Beyond the Mule's Path," *Pastoral Psychology* 69, no. 4 (August 2020): 357, https://doi.org/s11089-020-00921-6.

when he arrived Edward Kaplan, "A Jewish Dialogue with Howard Thurman: Mysticism, Compassion, and Community," *Cross Currents* 60, no. 4 (December 2010): 3.

"he encountered . . . and back to Life." Sue Bailey Thurman, epilogue to "Simmering on the Calm Presence and Profound Wisdom of Howard Thurman," special issue, *Debate and Understanding*, Spring 1982, 91, quoted in *The Papers of Howard Washington Thurman*, ed. Walter Earl Fluker, vol. 5, *The Wider Ministry, January 1963–April 1981* (Columbia, SC: University of South Carolina Press, 2019), xlii.